# WICCA

This book includes:

Wicca for Beginners

+

Wicca Spells

Wiccan for Beginners, Moon Rituals & Magic.

New Religion Starter Kit, Wheel Mystery and Witchcraft.

Wiccapedia for Solitary Practitioner.

# Table of Contents

TABLE OF CONTENTS ............................................................. 12

INTRODUCTION ..................................................................... 17

CHAPTER 1: DEFINITIONS AND HISTORY ......................... 19

CHAPTER 2: DEITIES ............................................................. 37

CHAPTER 3: ELEMENTS AND QUARTERS ......................... 55

CHAPTER 4: TOOLS OF THE TRADE .................................... 71

CHAPTER 5: THE WHEEL OF THE YEAR ............................ 84

CHAPTER 6: SABBATS .......................................................... 96

CHAPTER 7: ESBATS ............................................................ 120

CHAPTER 8: MAGIC AND THE BOOK OF SHADOWS ...... 137

CHAPTER 9: SOLITARY VS. COVEN ................................... 167

CONCLUSION ........................................................................ 169

WICCA SPELLS ...................................................................... 172

TABLE OF CONTENTS .......................................................... 174

INTRODUCTION ................................................................... 178

CHAPTER 1: THE ORIGINS OF WICCA ............................... 180

CHAPTER 2: WICCAN BELIEFS AND PRACTICES ............ 186

CHAPTER 3: THE TOOLS OF THE CRAFT ......................... 198

CHAPTER 4: THE GOD AND THE GODDESS ..................... 213

CHAPTER 5: THE ELEMENTS AND THE WHEEL OF THE YEAR ....................................................................................... 224

CHAPTER 6: SPELLS ............................................................ 257

CONCLUSION ...................................................................... 324

© Copyright 2019 by Rachel Herbs - All rights reserved.

The following Book is reproduced below with the goal of providing information that is as accurate and reliable as possible. Regardless, purchasing this Book can be seen as consent to the fact that both the publisher and the author of this book are in no way experts on the topics discussed within and that any recommendations or suggestions that are made herein are for entertainment purposes only. Professionals should be consulted as needed prior to undertaking any of the action endorsed herein.

This declaration is deemed fair and valid by both the American Bar Association and the Committee of Publishers Association and is legally binding throughout the United States.

Furthermore, the transmission, duplication, or reproduction of any of the following work including specific information will be considered an illegal act irrespective of if it is done electronically or in print. This extends to creating a secondary or tertiary copy of the work or a recorded copy and is only allowed with the express written consent from the Publisher. All additional right reserved.

The information in the following pages is broadly considered a truthful and accurate account of facts and as such, any inattention, use, or misuse of the information in question by the reader will render any resulting actions solely under their purview. There are no scenarios in which the publisher or the original

author of this work can be in any fashion deemed liable for any hardship or damages that may befall them after undertaking information described herein.

Additionally, the information in the following pages is intended only for informational purposes and should thus be thought of as universal. As befitting its nature, it is presented without assurance regarding its prolonged validity or interim quality. Trademarks that are mentioned are done without written consent and can in no way be considered an endorsement from the trademark holder.

# Wicca for Beginners

*Handbook for Elemental Magic, Herbal Magic with Nice Harmony. Wiccan Made Easy Guide for Solitary Practitioner with Spells. Wheel Mystery and Witchcraft for Beginners.*

# Table of Contents

TABLE OF CONTENTS ................................................................ 12

INTRODUCTION ...................................................................... 17

CHAPTER 1: DEFINITIONS AND HISTORY ......................... 19

CHAPTER 2: DEITIES ............................................................... 37

CHAPTER 3: ELEMENTS AND QUARTERS ......................... 55

CHAPTER 4: TOOLS OF THE TRADE ................................... 71

CHAPTER 5: THE WHEEL OF THE YEAR ........................... 84

CHAPTER 6: SABBATS ............................................................ 96

CHAPTER 7: ESBATS .............................................................. 120

CHAPTER 8: MAGIC AND THE BOOK OF SHADOWS ...... 137

CHAPTER 9: SOLITARY VS. COVEN .................................... 167

CONCLUSION ......................................................................... 169

© Copyright 2019 by Rachel Herbs - All rights reserved.

The following Book is reproduced below with the goal of providing information that is as accurate and reliable as possible. Regardless, purchasing this Book can be seen as consent to the fact that both the publisher and the author of this book are in no way experts on the topics discussed within and that any recommendations or suggestions that are made herein are for entertainment purposes only. Professionals should be consulted as needed prior to undertaking any of the action endorsed herein.

This declaration is deemed fair and valid by both the American Bar Association and the Committee of Publishers Association and is legally binding throughout the United States.

Furthermore, the transmission, duplication, or reproduction of any of the following work including specific information will be considered an illegal act irrespective of if it is done electronically or in print. This extends to creating a secondary or tertiary copy of the work or a recorded copy and is only allowed with the express written consent from the Publisher. All additional right reserved.

The information in the following pages is broadly considered a truthful and accurate account of facts and as such, any inattention, use, or misuse of the information in question by the reader will render any resulting actions solely under their purview. There are no scenarios in which the publisher or the original

author of this work can be in any fashion deemed liable for any hardship or damages that may befall them after undertaking information described herein.

Additionally, the information in the following pages is intended only for informational purposes and should thus be thought of as universal. As befitting its nature, it is presented without assurance regarding its prolonged validity or interim quality. Trademarks that are mentioned are done without written consent and can in no way be considered an endorsement from the trademark holder.

# Introduction

Congratulations on downloading *Wicca for Beginners* and thank you for doing so.

The following chapters will discuss everything that you'll need to know as a witch who's just starting out. We will dive into the ancient history of Paganism on which Wicca was founded, the modern history of Wicca in the 20th century, and the current state of the religion today.

This work will also dive into the divine archetypes worshipped in Wicca, with a special focus on the Lord and Lady, also known as the Triple Goddess and the Horned God. We will also have a brief overview of other deities sometimes worshipped in the Wiccan system. There will also be a chapter that describes the four elements and their meanings, and how you can use them to cast a magical circle.

There are many tools that are very important to this religion, such as the athame, the wand, the chalice, and the pentacle. We will dive into the symbolism of each of these tools, as well as how they can be placed on altars, and how they can be used in rituals. We will explore how those rituals take place on sacred festivals, as well as during the full moon.

Finally, this book will explore the use of magic, and the recording of spells in a personal Book of Shadows, as well as how to grow your practice as either a solitary practitioner or a member of a coven.

There are plenty of books on this subject on the market, thanks again for choosing this one! Every effort was made to ensure it is full of as much useful information as possible, please enjoy!

# Chapter 1: Definitions and History

Wicca is a modern religion based on an ancient system of spirituality practiced by indigenous Europeans for thousands of years. The ancient Europeans managed fantastic feats in the name of worship. They erected megalithic structures, such as Newgrange and Stonehenge; they had an intricate and complex knowledge of the stars and of celestial events, and they were keenly aware of the rhythms of the natural world.

# Ancient History

The ancient Europeans were experts in the rhythms of nature. In part, this was out of pure necessity. Due to the fact that this was an agrarian society, they lived and died by the turning of the seasons. One early frost or one late snowfall could spell disaster for the entire community. Being able to tune into and read the cycles of the seasons was vital for their very survival.

They had both reverence and fear for nature, as exemplified in the personification of many natural landmarks and features as beings or deities. For example, the Tuatha De Dannan, the pantheon of Ireland, translates to Children of the Goddess Danu. The great mother goddess Danu is named after the Danube River in mainland Europe; as settlers came over the sea to the British Isles, they brought with them their name for the great source of all life, Danu. The Danube River was the giver of life, providing sustenance and drinking water. Thus, the geographical feature of the river became the physical embodiment of the great mother goddess.

Another example of the close link that the ancient Europeans had with the natural world can be seen in how the ancient Irish had a three-way split in their cosmology in the form of Sky, Earth, and Sea. The number three was incredibly sacred to the ancient Celts, and the spirits and gods were each said to originate from one of the three realms. In the same way, each of those three realms was a source of both fear and life-giving sustenance for the ancients. They received fish from the sea, grain and crops from the land, and rain and water from the sky. They even believed in a host of other creatures—the sidhe, also known as the fae or faeries—who came from under the Earth and can cause havoc if not properly appeased.

The ancient Celts, who practice the form of Paganism upon which Wicca is most closely based, had many deities that were worshipped. These deities had many functions and were both male and female. These deities ruled over a vast array of functions, from weather to war, to agriculture, to healing, to the occult mysteries.

Some deities the ancients acknowledged had the power of the meteorological realms. Without the advanced weather-monitoring systems that we have today, the weather was largely unknown to them. They would acknowledge and worship many different kinds of weather deities to gain boons and safe passage.

War was another huge aspect of ancient life, with fiefdoms, kingdoms, and clans constantly going to war with one another. Groups were constantly encroaching on each other's borders for one reason or another—whether a lack of resources or a simple desire for territorial expansion. War deities were called on to help achieve victory.

When someone fell and broke a bone in ancient Europe, there was no hospital to go to. Oftentimes, a broken bone or simple accident could be a death sentence. Deities in the healing realm were invoked to help the wounded person mend, and to return to wellness. To ensure against these accidents and the woes of everyday life, deities that acted as protectors—whether of the household, of travelers, of animals, etc.—were also often invoked.

From a purely materialist and psychological point of view, it would make sense that the ancients would worship these deities. Attributing actions to the gods, who could be prayed to and supplicated, gave them a sense of control in a dangerous and largely uncertain world. From a spiritual perspective, they looked to the natural world and saw the magic and power inherent in it, and devised ways to connect to it.

These deities were worshipped in a great many ways. People sought to connect with them to ensure that the gods were appeased and that the people had their blessings. Perhaps the most impressive of these worship sites are Stonehenge, Newgrange, and the standing stones at Sternness. The oldest of these, the standing stones at Sternness, has several astrological links and marks the position of the sun and moon at various points throughout the years. The sites at Newgrange and Stonehenge also align with the astronomical realm, in this case, the solstice sun. There is evidence of complex rituals being conducted at these places, including pottery, herbs, food offerings, and the bones of many kinds of animals.

It is an often-forgotten truth that the ancient Europeans engaged in sacrifice. Often it was the sacrifice of part of the harvest to the gods, or particularly prized livestock. However, human sacrifice was also not unheard of. It wasn't just the ancient Mesoamericans that engaged in this practice; indigenous Europeans engaged in this practice as well. If something was of particularly high value a community, then it would make sense that they would offer that thing of highest value to the gods. By offering things of great value, they hoped to receive great boons in return.

Oftentimes the gods were attributed particularly fickle and humanlike personas. If they felt slighted by an inadequate offering, they could reproach their followers by sending disaster. Therefore, it wasn't a spirit of cruelty that led them to sacrifice living animals, or even people, to the deities. Rather, it was simply the deeply ingrained desire for survival.

There were a select few that were attributed special connection to the gods. These were known as awenyddion, priests, and Druids. These people interceded with the deities on behalf of the people, letting the community know the will of the deities.

Once the will of the gods was known, these leaders would then officiate ritual ceremonies and offerings on the behalf of the community.

The relationship of the ancients to the gods was intimate and intense, just as their relationship with the natural world was intimate and intense. It was not this way by intention, but by necessity. The rhythms and flows of nature—and therefore, the doings of the gods—affected them on a daily basis, and had a huge impact on whether or not they would live or die.

## Modern History

Modern Wicca was founded in 1954 by Gerald Brosseau Gardener. He was born in 1884 to an upper-middle-class family in England in Lancashire. Gardener spent much of his childhood in the autonomous region of Portugal, called Madeira. He was something of an amateur archaeologist and anthropologist. He spent much of his adult life in Asia, where he became familiar with a wide variety of occult and esoteric traditions. He spent time with the indigenous peoples of Malaya, and in the spirit of amateur anthropology, described their magical traditions.

He read widely, and among his influences were the writings of the infamous Aleister Crowley. When he returned to England shortly prior to the beginning of World War II, he became intimately involved with the local occult community. He joined the Rosicrucian Order Crotona Fellowship, an esoteric community. Through the Fellowship, he met and was initiated into the New Forest Coven.

The members of the Rosicrucian Order Crotona Fellowship looked down on New Forest Coven, despite the fact that they were a sub-sect of the same order. The New Forest Coven consisted of members who were not considered "noble," and who had to work for a living. While the other members of the Fellowship were serious and austere, the members of the New Forest Coven were described as genial and friendly. Gardener quickly befriended its members and joined their ranks.

Gardener believed this coven to be a surviving pre-Christian witchcraft tradition and made it his mission to revitalize the faith. Modern evidence, however, points to the New Forest Coven having been founded sometime in the 1930s.

While working with the New Forest Coven, he participated in an initiation ceremony in which he was made to strip naked and then inducted into the order. He also participated in a rite in which they raised a "cone of power" mean to prevent the Nazis from invading Britain.

Gardener supplemented the New Forest Coven's already-existing rituals with ideas he derived from Freemasonry, the writings of Crowley, and ceremonial magic. He combined all of these things together into what would become known as Gardnerian Wicca.

Wanting to spread ensures the tradition did not die out; Gardener went on to found the Bricket Wood Coven in 1946. He also had a growing interest in nudism and purchased a plot of land called Bricket Wood that would become a nudist colony. It is after this plot of land that the coven took its name. It was at Bricket Wood that Gardener began to work with Doreen Valiente, who became a high priestess. Valiente began to shift focus away from sole worship of the Horned God back to emphasizing the Goddess. She also helped to write the famed Charge of the Goddess.

She also helped to rewrite the portions of the coven's Book of Shadows (magical grimoire) that had been lifted wholesale from Aleister Crowley's Thelema tradition. Despite her major contributions to the coven and to the history of Wicca, she and Gardener had a falling-out; Valiente went on to found her own coven, while Gardener remained with Bricket Wood.

Gardener continued to initiate new members, and Bricket Wood grew in size and esteem. His students went off to form their own covens, practicing what was had been coined as "Gardnerian Wicca." Coverage from the press was in turns bemused and horrified; the former painting the coven as a group of eccentric nature enthusiasts, and the latter deeming them as slavering devil-worshippers.

This era in history was haunted by the memory of the First World War, yet also covered in the shadow of the second looming World War. It was also emerging from the stuffiness and restriction of Victorian England, an era which ended at the turn of the 20th century in 1901. There was a newfound sense of experimentalism and a loosening of moral restriction. However, there was also the sense of imminent danger brought on by the fighting superpowers all about the world.

Other ceremonial magic traditions were also on the rise, including Druidry and Freemasonry. In part, the 20th-century blossoming of Wicca was due to the seeds planted in the 18th century Romanticism movement, which glorified the pre-Iron Age Celtic peoples. Groups calling themselves "Druid" gathered and began to perform ceremonial magic, although most identified as Christian and their rituals were largely based on Freemasonry.

The gardener was growing more and more connected to the witchcraft tradition during a time when society at large was also infatuated with the spiritualist mysteries—and also growing largely disillusioned with those mysteries. In the 18th century, it was considered the height of fashion for upper-class persons to host spiritualist mediums at parties in their homes. These "mediums" and others of their ilk were by and large showmen, rather than genuine mouthpieces of the divine.

The ruse was uncovered often, and eventually, disillusionment began to pervade the public consciousness. For example, Harry Houdini was obsessed with exposing spiritual frauds. So, while there was a growing yearning for spiritual connection, society was growing disenchanted and cynical.

Gardener sought to tap into that seeking spirit. With the repeal of England's archaic Witchcraft Laws in 1951, he was finally free to spread his tradition without fear of legal prosecution.

The movement gained great steam in the 1960s. This was the decade of the counter-culture when youths were expanding their consciousness by rejecting authority, ingesting psychedelic drugs, or both. They were shucking off the constraints of the tight-laced 1950s, and getting back to nature. Wicca, which claimed to be descended from pre-Christian witchcraft traditions, called to these young peoples by promising to let them tune in with nature.

Though Gerald Gardener died in 1964, his movement was only just beginning. The 1960s were the decade that would see his tradition spread across the world. In 1963, a man named Raymund Buckland was inducted into Gardnerian Wicca and then went home to New York to found the first American coven, the Long Island Coven. From there, it spread across the world.

# Wicca Today

Wicca has truly blossomed across the world. In the year 1990, there were about 8000 Wiccans in the United States. As of 2008, there were 340,000. As the decades have rolled on, the numbers of people adhering to the Wiccan faith has grown exponentially. In just two decades, the number of people practicing faith increased over 42-fold. And they haven't stopped growing.

As of 2018, a grand total of 1.5 million people listed their religion as either "Wiccan" or more generally as "Pagan" in a research survey. "Pagan" is the umbrella term under which Wicca falls. This umbrella shelters other paths, such as Druidry, Reconstructionism (such as those worshiping Egyptian or Greek pantheons), and Alchemical traditions. The number of people practicing nature-centric faiths has exploded in since their revival in the early part of the 20th century.

There are many reasons that more and more people are flocking to Wicca and these other Pagan traditions. There is increasing dissatisfaction with the mainstream Abrahamic faiths of Judaism, Islam, and Christianity. However, by and large, most converts to Wicca and Paganism come from a Christian background.

There is also an increasing awareness of our intimate links with the natural world, and the way we affect, and are affected by it. A growing awareness of pollution, climate change, and the ozone layer has led many people to a more empathetic ecological consciousness. This eco-focused consciousness not only informs their activism but can be viewed as causing them to seek a mystical connection with nature.

Though the original incarnation was Gardnerian Wicca, there have been many schools and lineages that have come into existence over the past century. As the number of adherents has grown and diversified, so too have the kinds of Wicca. These other lineages include the Alexandrian, Celtic, Dianic, and Eclectic.

Alexandrian Wicca is a slightly more liberal sister to Gardnerian Wicca. It heavily emphasizes the male-female duality. In terms of ceremonial structure, they are very similar, with some slight differences in the elemental association. The cycle of their rituals is heavily focused on the Holly King, who rules the winter, and his cycle with the Oak King, who rules the summer.

Dianic Wicca gives primacy to the Goddess in their worship. There are two branches; the first, called Old Dianic, has covens that are made up of both men and women. The second, called Feminist Dianic Witchcraft, are women-only groups. Men are banned, and this second group has often been accused of transphobia for not allowing Trans women to participate in their rituals.

Celtic Wicca is also known as the Church of Wicca. By and large, they have been the most active publicly visible of the Wiccan groups, especially in the early days of the 1990s. Their ritual structure contains elements of Celtic traditions, based on a framework of ceremonial and high magic.

Finally, Eclectic Wicca rounds out the list. This variety of Wicca was founded in the 1960s. The hallmark of this tradition is the flexibility that it allows its adherents. Followers of Eclectic Wicca are able to take aspects from many traditions and faiths to meet their needs. They can incorporate ancient Celtic deities, a Catholic invocation of a saint, and a Gardnerian structure all within the same ritual.

There are many notable modern Wiccan and Pagan groups. These include Circle Sanctuary; The Pagan Federation; and the Order of Bards, Ovates, and Druids. These organizations have worked tirelessly to ensure that not only the spiritual tradition continues, but also that its practitioners can practice safely and openly without fear of retribution.

Up until fairly recent history, it was extremely common for practitioners of Wicca to be fired from their jobs, denied opportunities, and harassed by local communities on the basis of their faith. To this day, some fundamentalist groups still attempt to encroach on the religious freedom of Wiccans and Pagans.

In recent history, many great leaps and bounds have been made. Pagan Advocacy Groups such as the Lady Liberty League have formed a branch of legal defense for Wiccans and Pagans who find themselves discriminated against. Wiccans and Pagans today enjoy a far greater level of safety and freedom in the workplace and in their communities.

Wicca and Paganism have grown to be one of the largest minority religions in the United States. While they do not come anywhere near the number of adherents as Christianity, Wicca and Paganism have numbers of adherents similar to Sikhism and Hinduism in the USA. They are a significant chunk of the American demographic.

With grown numbers have come growing public acknowledgment, and greater rights. In 2006 an army chaplain named Captain Don Larsen was dismissed after requesting to become the first Wiccan military chaplain. Despite an exemplary record of service, he was dismissed. However, in 2007, things began to change in relation to the military. Spearheaded by Selena Fox of Circle Sanctuary, a lawsuit was settled; this settlement finally allowed the pentacle to be a symbol engraved on military headstones. Since 2007 many other Pagan symbols have been added, including Thor's hammer and the Druidic Awen, among others.

Wiccan and Pagan chaplains are now readily available in the military, as well as in places such as prisons. The freedom to have access to the ministers, rituals and symbols of one's faith has finally come around to include these ancestral religions.

The tradition of Wicca was based on the spirit of indigenous European religions tens of thousands of years old. This spirit was recaptured and reimagined by Gerald Gardner, who helped to reignite the light of witchcraft for the modern age. Today, Wicca and Paganism are one of the largest minority faiths in the USA, and it will surely only keep growing from here on out.

# Chapter 2: Deities

Now that we've spent some time on the history and origin of the Wiccan faith, we can dive into the main deities worshipped in this religion. Wicca is a very dualistic religion, with a heavy emphasis on the division between the feminine and masculine archetypes. The feminine archetype is worshipped as the Goddess, and the masculine archetype is worshipped as the Horned God. Though the two energies are divided into separate deities, it is the unification of these two energies that is one of the most highly revered forms of magic in Wicca. When the inseminating Horned One activates the creative potential in the Goddess's womb, new life is created.

# The Goddess

The Goddess is the creative wellspring of life. She is divided into three categories, represented by the phases of the moon. These phases are waxing, full, and waning. The waxing or growing aspect of the Goddess is known as the Maiden. The center phase is known as the Mother. And the waning phase is known as the Crone. These three energies represent the three archetypal energies that most women will engage with at some point in their life.
*Goddess as Maiden*

The Goddess in this aspect is associated with the time of spring. The plants are beginning to shoot forth new buds and are wearing flowers. The year is young and full of vibrancy and the primacy of life. So too is the Maiden. She walks through the Wildwood with flowers in her hair, exuding the exuberant energy of the young year.

The Maiden is an emblem of youth. She exudes energy and childlike wonder. She is a beacon of innocence that has not yet been tempered by experience or burdened with the weight of the world. The eagerness and awe with which she approaches reality is an important reminder for practitioners who have grown bitter and world-weary. She reminds them to take a fresh perspective and to appreciate anew the world around them.

She is also a wellspring of creativity. She is young and fiery, eager to try new things and to get her hands dirty. The Goddess in this aspect wishes to leave no stone unturned, no mountain is unclimbed, no path unwalked. In this willingness to explore the novel and new, she is able to use her awestruck perspective and boundless energy to translate her inner thoughts into creative action.

The Maiden is as-yet unfettered by the responsibilities of home, hearth, and husband. Though unmarried, she is not necessarily a virgin. She is free from the demands of children and household, and as such she is able to expend her nurturing energy on growing herself and her life. That independence allows to travel and explore, to experiment and take risks—all things that have a family prevents one from doing easily. Being unwed also allows the Maiden to explore her inner landscapes as well as her outer landscapes. This is the time for self-discovery and inner transformation.

## *Goddess as* Mother

The Goddess in this aspect serves as the portal through which new life enters the world. Everyone has a mother. Through the harrowing, painful process of childbirth, she pushes her children forward into life. Though she suffers to open the portal, once her children arrive, she is filled with a love so boundless that it is often beyond words.

The Goddess in this phase is a nurturing figure. Mothers suckle their children at their breast, redirect them away from dangerous situations, and otherwise invest time, energy, and effort into their children's development. She is like a gardener carefully planting seeds, ensuring that they get enough sun and water so that they can blossom and grow.

Mothers are also not only stewards of children but leaders of households. Even in less liberated times when women were constrained to the home, in the home, the woman ruled supreme. She arranged matters of the household, oversaw the staff, and ensured that all of the needs of the inhabitants were met. She is the master of logistics.

Not only is she the matriarch, but she is also a queen. For what are queens but the mothers of their countries? Their subjects are their children, and they have a duty to serve them with the utmost of respect, humility, and ability. Good queens give their very life and soul in service to their people, as mothers give everything of themselves for their children.

And of course, there is the greatest mother of all, Mother Earth. Gaia is the mother to us all. It is from her that we gained the nutrients that helped us grow in the womb, her skin is what we walk upon, and she is the dust to which we will one day return. Mother Earth is the first mother, the mother of mothers. She is the origin of the human race.

## *Goddess as Crone*

Once a woman has reached the end of her fertile years, menopause ensues. During this phase, she moves from the active part of life into a more reflective time. The Goddess in this aspect symbolizes harvesting the wisdom of one's life to discern a distill its lessons and truths. She is the elder of the community that advises the community leaders. She mediates disputes, settles scores, and provides valuable insight. Through her, the tribe accesses their long history, ensuring that they do not make the same mistakes. The Crone is invoked for wisdom.

The Goddess in this phase is also straddling the line between life and death. As she grows older, she grows closer to the veil. Being closer to the veil, she is able to peer through and see into the realm of the spirits. Being able to peer beyond allows the Crone to act as a guide for those who are dying. She serves as a guide to the beyond and can help steer the spirits of the departed on their way to the afterlife.

She stands at the gateway, and in places in-between. It is an archetypal experience to meet the Crone as the Crossroads. She already has one foot between life and death, and thus easily manifests in places that are halfway in and out of the veil. She is the deity that manifests at the threshold and stands at the doorway to the spirit world.

Finally, the Crone is also associated with the mysterious old woman who lives out in the forest, alone. Some associate her with the Wicked Witch. She is a recluse who keeps to herself, who may be painted as evil by the local townspeople—this is where stories like Hansel and Gretel come from. Baba Yaga fits into this mold, the Old Russian fairy tale witch whose magical house wanders around the woods on chicken feet.

# God

The counterpart to the Goddess is God. The Goddess represents the yin, or still principle. God represents the yang or active principle. He is movement, power, and strength. The male physical form tends to have greater muscle mass, and thus a larger amount of physical power.

## *Wild Man*

If the Goddess has dominion over the home and community, God lives in wild places. Everywhere that is untamed, overgrown, and green is his home. He is the lord of the wildwood. He is often depicted with antlers or horns. There are many ancient depictions of horned gods. The Gundestrup Cauldron, an ancient piece of mystical artwork from Denmark, depicts such a figure. He sits cross-legged, commanding the animals that stand around him.

The Horned God is also often depicted as being made of leaves and bark and plants, with his face emerging from the greenery. He is not only the king of the green world; he is the green world itself. He is not only the lord of the animals; with the antlers sprouting from his head, he lives within the animals.

He is also the god of the hunt. When the sound of dogs baying on the wind is heard, he can be found. He lives in the heat of the chase between the predator and its prey. Though it may seem counterintuitive that one being could be embodied in both elements, both energies are actually just two sides of the same coin.

In the wild, animals must consume each other to survive. The rabbit eats the grass, and the hawk eats the rabbit. Each is simply an expression of nature's energy, flowing from one into the other. They are not separated from each other but united in the ceaseless cycles of survival. This is the embodiment of the Horned God.

The God, as consort to the Goddess, also takes on the role of the lover. No matter how fierce and powerful a man may be, he reveals his tenderness and gentleness when with his partner. His power is not dominating, but rather supporting. He does not rule over the Goddess but stands next to her as an equal. Theirs is a true partnership; each is equal yet distinct from the other.

God is also standing in the role of protector. He stands tall and ready with his shield, all of the power of the wild behind him. There is a reason that most of the deities associated with war are men. Men were soldiers, captains, and warriors in ancient times. It was their job to defend their tribe or their country, and thus by extension, their families.

There is another expression of the dualism found in the Goddess and God, from Eastern philosophy. That expression is that of the yin-yang. The yin is the principle of stillness, receptivity, and quiet. The yang is the principle of movement, providing, and action. These two concepts work well when applied to the Lord and Lady.

The Goddess embodies yin, the feminine half of this energy. The God embodies yang, the masculine half of this energy. Together they represent the totality of creation, one feeding into the other. The yang God energy is the engine that drives the movement. He is the power of the spear, the strength of the shield, the life of the animals, and the flourishing of the natural world.

## *Embodying the Year*

Because God has such a close link with the natural world, he also embodies its cycles and seasons. The life cycle of the year is mirrored by his journey through the phases of life. He relives the cycle of birth, life, death, and rebirth year after year, season after season.

Yule is the longest night of the year, and it can also be accurately thought of like the darkness of the womb. The God died at Samhain and entered the darkness of the tomb. Here the tomb transforms to the womb, the darkness of the grave transmuting into the darkness of the generative birth waters.

When the sun dawns, after a full half-year of waning and shortening days, it marks the period when the days begin to lengthen again. Ancestrally, this has been regarded as the birth of the sun. At this time, God is a shining newborn baby reborn from the womb of the Goddess.

The God enters into youth as the year begins to reawaken with the springtime. With the natural world begins to put forward flowers and greenery, God enters the phase of a child, exploring the world with open-eyed curiosity. This part of the year is demarcated by the holidays of Imbolc and Ostara.

Springtime is when the animals and plants are full of vigor and life. Just as children have seemingly endless amounts of energy, so the natural world is full of incredible business. Animals are building their nests, laying eggs, and rearing their young. The baby animals found everywhere throughout the natural world are the counterparts of God.

As the year rounds toward summer and the natural world mature, so does the God. The young animals are growing to full strength, and the plants have shed their flowers and come out in full leaf. The summer season is demarcated by the holidays of Beltane, Litha, and Lammas.

By this time of the year, the deer have fully grown their antlers. They began to grow in March, but they will be fully grown by the end of June. Stags are the animal representation of the Horned God, who sprouts a majestic pair of antlers from the crown of his head. As the deer mature, so too by this time have many of the other small animals grown to maturity and left the den. Rabbits have become fully grown and left the warren, and birds have fledged and left the nest to strike out on their own. At this time, God stands at the height of his strength and power.

The autumn is associated with the decline. It is overshadowed with the looming form of winter. It is a time of gathering and hoarding, as the natural world becomes increasingly aware of the declines all around them. This is representative of the time of old age and the harvest holidays of Mabon and Samhain.

The leaves are falling off of the trees as they prepare for the death of winter. Humans and animals harvest the bounty of the natural world. As we harvest his body, God naturally begins to decline into old age. As the natural world prepares for winter, he does too. Once the final leaf falls from the tree, God dies with the winter. He is reborn again at Yule, at the winter solstice.

## The Goddess and God by Other Names

### *The God*

The Horned God has had many faces throughout history and through many cultures. He has appeared in Ireland and Denmark, all the way across Europe to Greece and Rome. He is venerated under many labels, though any of his names can be used to invoke his spirit.

One of God's names is Cernunnos. This deity is a Celtic god of life, animals, fertility, wealth, and the underworld. Though his name only appears once, his imagery appears all over northern Europe. The figure on the Gunderstrup Cauldron is typically named as Cernunnos. The antlered god figure appears among all of the Celtic peoples of mainland Europe and the British Isles, and as far west as the Iberian Peninsula and southern Spain.

Another name for God is Pan. Pan is a god of ancient Greek mythology. He too is a god of the wild places and the untamed lands. He is also the god of shepherds and flocks, who foray into the wilds. Pan is especially fond of the mountains of Greece, as well as of improvised music and parties.

Pan not only has horns, but also the torso, legs, and feet of a goat. He is a manifestation of God's energy as a Lover to the Goddess. Pan is a deity that is known for his sexual prowess and appetite. He takes many lovers and is considered to be quite virile. He is often considered a god of wooded glens, fields, and groves, for these are the locations where it is said he would take his lovers.

Faunus is the Roman interpretation of the god Pan. However, there are a few slight differences between the two deities. Faunus is the deity of plains and fields, and he is especially associated with cattle, and causing them to become fertile. Like Pan, Faunus is a horned deity, who has the hindquarters, legs, and hooved feet of a goat.

Faunus is considered to be one of the oldest Roman deities, worshipped far back into antiquity; he is also considered an elder among the gods. Faunus had an oracle oat the sacred grove of Tibur; when kings and other people of import needed a glimpse into the future, they would consult with the Horned God's oracle.

A final incarnation of the Horned God is as the Green Man. The Green Man is an ancient motif found across Europe through many ages across thousands of years. He is found everywhere from ancient Pagan sacred sites to the carvings of churches.

The Green Man is literally a man's face made of leaves. This is the form of the God that is one with the Wildwood, which lives inside of the plants and animals. God rises and falls with the yearly cycles of nature, and here is represented as such. He is such a universal archetype that many theorize that he developed across multiple European cultures, which all converged to provide us with the image we know today.

## *The Goddess*

There are ancient examples of a great Earth Mother figure being venerated across the world. Some of the oldest examples of art come from ancient cultures that worshipped a rotund, fertile mother-figure. The Venus of Willendorf is one such example. In ancient times, starvation was a very real concern. Rarely anyone was able to compile enough resources to gain very much weight.

Thus, such a rotund figure was a sign of not only prosperity and abundance, but also of fertility. The figure has the large, ample hips of someone who is capable of bearing many children. Her engorged, oversized breasts speak of the ability to produce prodigious amounts of milk and to nourish many babies. The Goddess figure represents the way that the Earth nourishes her children.

The Goddess is not only associated with the Earth, but also with the Moon. The moon is the primary representation in Wicca of the Maiden Mother Crone dynamic, due to the way that she waxes and wanes. When the moon is just past new and is still a crescent, it is representative of the Maiden. She has not yet grown to her full power, but she is growing in brightness.

When the moon is full, the Goddess is at her full power as the Mother. The swollen moon is reminiscent of the pregnant woman's swollen belly. This time in the lunar cycle represents the full fruiting of woman's potential to bring new life into the world. It also represents the time when the moon has the greatest effect over the tides.

Finally, when the moon is waning, she is representative of the Goddess in her aspect as the Crone. The waning moon is past her peak, and will eventually diminish with her death at the dark moon. So too the Crone is no longer at full strength, and spends much of her time in the growing dark, walking the path of shadows.

The Goddess is also associated with the sea and the ocean. This is because water is the emotional realm, over which the Goddess presides. She holds sway over the waters of the subconscious mind, and navigates them with patience, love, and tenderness, as a mother helps her children navigate their emotions.

The sea and ocean are also emblematic of the water of the womb. All babies are suspended in the amniotic fluid prior to birth, and it is this liquid that shields and protects us as we grow and develop. The Goddess lives in these waters, using the water of life to help protect and nourish her children. As a final note, the moon controls the sea, and the Goddess presides over both dominions.

The Goddess and God are the principal deities of Wicca. They are known by many names and hold sway over many areas. However, they have a consistent and powerful presence, despite their diversity. The active power of God hunts through the wildwood, growing and dying each year. The power of the Goddess lives eternally in the Earth, the Moon, and the Sea, and relives the Maiden Mother Crone cycle each month with the waxing and waning of the moon.

# Chapter 3: Elements and Quarters

One of the most important parts of Wicca is the idea of the four quarters and their four associated elements. It is important to understand the symbolism and meaning behind these so that you are able to cast your own magical circles and to carry out your own rituals. The spirit of each of the four cardinal directions is honored in Wicca, as are the four elements. North is associated with Earth. East is associated with Air. The South is associated with Fire. Finally, the West is associated with Water. Learning to work with these elemental and directional archetypes is vital to the aspiring Wiccan ritualist.

# Earth in the North

The direction of "north" often brings a host of images to people's minds: cold winds, tundra, caribou, cold, and winter. Oftentimes, people's imagination wanders up to the North Pole. It is generally true that the farther north you go, the colder it gets. In Alaska, some places only get up to sixty degrees on their hottest summer day.

This direction is associated with the element of Earth. Even in the farthest north, when the spring arrives, even the coldest tundra bursts into bloom. The caribou give birth, the birds migrate home to nest, and the season of plenty begins. The element of Earth is associated with growth in the wild, with new leaves and flowers abounding. Anything that roots into the ground and produces leaves is especially linked to the element of Earth.

The element of Earth is not only associated with the springtime but the plant and animal worlds in general, especially animals that feed upon vegetation and plants. The fertility of plants and animals is a representation of this element is flowing and abundant.

North is also associated with the ancestors, as is the element of Earth. On a purely physical level, the bodies of our ancestors are buried beneath the ground. Their bodies have returned to the soil, and so they live on within the element of Earth. On a spiritual level, the ancestors are said in many traditions to dwell in a pleasant underworld, beneath the ground.

The wisdom that ancestors bring is ancient and weathered, having been tried and tested through many seasons. It can be compared to an ancient and weathered stone. The stone is worn by wind and rain, refined, rough edges worn away by many seasons. So does the experience of the ancestor's shape and form their wisdom, refining it through the years into a valuable resource.

This element is also known to be steady and unmoving. While in its negative expression it can bring forward stubbornness and unwillingness to change, in a positive expression, this element can be an anchor. It is steadfast and unyielding. A great stone can stand for millions of years. It is only through an almost inconceivable span of time that it can be worn away. It is solid, permanent, and reliable. It represents the human trait of unwavering resolve.

When someone is feeling unsteady, vulnerable, and uprooted, it can be beneficial to tap into and visualize the attributes of the element of Earth. Being able to visualize yourself as a strong, unwavering stone can give you the resolve that you need to make it through difficult circumstances. Just as stones are able to stand through the mightiest storm, so too can you stand strong through the whirlwind forces that may move through your life.

The element of Earth is also linked to trees and plants, and especially to their roots. The roots of trees dig down deep into the soil, which is also the domain of this element. Roots meet soil in order to bring it water and nutrients that it needs in order to survive. The roots of the tree also serve to stabilize the tree, letting it stand tall and remain upright even in high winds. Just like the stone, it is able to stand tall due to its connection with the element of Earth, even in the most challenging of circumstances. Trees are also literally associated with "putting down roots." When someone seeks to establish their home and family, this is also the domain of the element of Earth.

Caves are also emblematic of this element. They are physically an entrance into the Earth, and many cultures revered caves as entrances into the underworld. They are made of stone and crack with earth open wide. The darkness and stillness found in caves are also held within this element.

All the other elements are dynamic, and have movement in their nature to at least some degree. Water flows, the wind blows, and the fire flickers. Earth alone holds steady. The stillness and darkness that Earth embodies can be likened to the darkness that a seed feels once it has been implanted in the soil. Though many fear the darkness and feel smothered by it, in reality, the darkness is also the place in which seeds are planted, and in which they grow. Though the Earth holds the spirit of the darkness, it is not darkness to be feared; rather it is nurturing darkness, of growth, like the womb.

# The air in the East

In the direction of the east lives the element of Air. The east is most notably associated with the direction of the rising sun. When the new day breaks, the sun's first rays light up the horizon with a brilliant array of colors. The east signifies new beginnings, new light, and new opportunities. Just as the darkness of the night is illuminated by the sunshine of a new day, so is the darkness of life enlivened by the dawning of new possibilities. The wind and Air live in this direction, are summoned when you call this quarter of the circle.

The most noticeable manifestation of the element of Air is the wind. It moves everywhere, ceaselessly, across every continent, ocean, lake, and sea. It is forever in motion. Air is perhaps the most restless of all the elements and can be considered to stand in opposition to the element of Earth, whose traits are steadfastness and immobility. Air is always in motion, and there is a reason that forces of transformation are often referred to as "the winds of change." When they blow through your life, new things are coming.

The inward manifestation of the element of Air is the breath. As humans take in air through the mouth and nose, it swirls down into the lungs, where oxygen is extracted. The breath is the element of air circulating through our bodies to provide our bodies with the oxygen we need. We as humans require the element of Air on the most fundamental level; without it, in mere minutes we would begin to suffocate. Learning to breathe deeply allows us to calm intense mental and emotional storms, as well as gain insight and mental clarity.

When the element of Air moves out of our lungs and is shaped by our mouths, it becomes communication. Speaking and listening are caught up with this element, as the vibrations, we cause in the air move from our mouths to the listener's ears. Just as birds fly on the wind, so too do ideas move back and forth on the element of Air. Language is an astounding human capacity that enables us to transfer mental constructs from one person's inner world to the mind of another.

Just as the capacity of communication is related to the element of Air, so too is the capacity of understanding. When someone speaks to us and plants an idea in our mind using their power of the breath and Air, our capacity to comprehend the idea is sparked by this element. Thoughts are words that take place in the mind; language and speech are inherently a part of Air. When someone expresses themselves thoughtfully and carefully, and the idea moves into the mind gracefully, we are able to understand.

When someone is communicating with you, and you are seeking to understand their words, it is also natural that you would focus in on the element of truth. Truth and clarity are associated with Air. A useful symbol is to consider the eagle. The eagle flies high on the back of the win and has an amazing vision that can see prey almost a mile down. Being able to discern things at such a distance is a superpower; that power is linked with the ability to discern the truth of a statement or action is related.

Just as truth is linked to the element of air, so too is the nature of the human mind. The human self could be said to be composed of four elements. The physical body is made of Earth. The emotional body is made up of Water. The spiritual fire or animating force is Fire. And the mental capacity for thought is Air. Air drives the mind and gives us the power for rational thought and expression, to see and understand the truth, and to communicate with one another.

The ability to communicate is also what has given humanity one of our greatest gifts: the power of story, song, and poetry. The vocal arts are some of the oldest known to man. While humans began painting on cave walls some twenty thousand years ago, we have been using the vocal arts for far longer. The urge to gather around fires and sing songs and tell stories is one of the most primal human urges. It dates back to the dawn of our species. Thus, Air is the domain of singers, poets, storytellers, and musicians.

## Fire in the South

When people think of the direction of "south," they often think of warmth, with beaches and palm trees. It is true that the closer you get to the equator, the warmer it becomes. That heat is associated with the element of Fire.

Fire is perhaps the trickiest elements. All of the other elements follow certain forms and are somewhat predictable in their natures. Fire, though, must be handled with the utmost care. Earth is solid; Water is a liquid; Air is a gas; Fire is plasma. This is the most volatile state of matter. All of the other elements have their own inherent existence. Fire only exists for a brief moment as a chemical reaction between oxygenated air and burnable material; it must be constantly maintained, but also guarded to prevent it from running amok.

There is a reason that it is referred to as the "spark" of inspiration. When people feel the blossoming of the creative urge inside, it is like a fire. It catches hold of their mind and spreads to become an all-consuming flame. Creativity is the primal engine of creation. It is an active generation. The fire of the sun causes the flourishing of life on Earth and the proliferation of plants and animals. The fire of creativity causes the flourishing of human life, and the proliferation of music, art, poetry, stories, dance, and all other art forms.

Fire is also one of the most volatile elements. On the one hand, it was integral to the evolution of humankind. Without mastering fire and gaining the ability to cook our food, we wouldn't have been able to grow our brains to such a large degree. Fires warm our hearts and help us survive through the winter. However, the fire must be treated with respect. When mishandled, it can burn the tender. Or worse, if it gets out of control, it can turn into a wildfire. Wildfires can destroy forests, homes, and anything in its path. Fire out of control is a truly terrifying sight to behold.

But when the fire is carefully tended, it can be an immensely powerful tool. Ancient scientists used fires in the processes of alchemy and blacksmithing. In both cases, the element of fire is used to transform one thing into another. In alchemy, lead is transformed into gold. In blacksmithing, useless hunks of metal are transformed into weapons, household goods, and incredibly helpful tools. The fire has a great power to help, and also to transform. Fire helps to purify these metals and to eliminate impurities. Meditating on the element of Fire can help you to burn away things that no longer serve you, and to transform your life.

When the fire is lit within someone, it can take the form of sexual energy and sexual drive. There's a reason that love is often described as "hot" and "steamy." Fire manifests as physical desire and lust. The passion that enters new relationships is related to the element of Fire. However, just like real fires, these flames have to be tended wisely. Otherwise, people can end up getting hurt or burned if the emotions are not carefully looked after. Similarly, anger is an emotional expression of Fire. It needs to be carefully reigned in and managed, or it can lash and out and burn.

When properly managed, Fire can be a desperately needed guiding light. When someone is lost, they are often described as being "in the dark." The world seems like a black, lonely place, and they are often searching for a way out. Meditating on fire can help someone to light the fire they need to lead them out of the darkness. When someone is afraid and lost, Fire is represented in the light at the end of the tunnel, manifesting to show them the way out.

Fire is also emblematic of willpower and personal strength. When someone is a powerful, charismatic leader, they are often described as "glowing." The inner light that they exude is a manifestation of the element of Fire. Their inner light is bright as they seek to take the reins of their own destiny and to lead. It can be very difficult to let yourself to do something—just as it can be difficult to start a fire on wet wood. However, once the fire is lit, the driving engine begins to churn, and changes are made.

Fire is also representative of life itself. It is representative of the element of Spirit and is the driving force that animates all life. All animals and plants and beings are filled with the driving fire. It is the most ephemeral and mysterious of the elements. Someone can be full of fire and life, and dead the next day. The only difference is that the fire has gone out, and the spark has left them.

## Water in the West

The west is the direction of the sunset. It is the direction of endings and of letting go, as the day let's goes of the sun to bring in the night. On the North American continent, the western part of the continent is bounded by the Pacific Ocean, the largest ocean on Earth. It is in this direction that the element of Water lives. Water is the most mysterious of the four elements. It is constantly in motion like Air, but is more opaque, with darker depths and more complex and mystifying tides and patterns. The magical properties of water have mystified our ancestors for tens of thousands of years.

The seas and oceans are some of the most unexplored places on the planet. We know more about the surface of the moon than we do about the bottoms of our own oceans. There are forms of life that live below the surface of which we know nothing, and virtually every time a submersible goes down to the bottom of the Marianas Trench, they find some kind of new species. This mystery that surrounds the element of Water makes it an apt metaphor for the human subconscious. Try as we might understand the inner workings of our unconscious minds, there are many things that live beneath the surface; we can only learn so much with each submarine trip into the deep. Water is also linked with the emotional aspect of the self. Oftentimes, emotions rise up from the deepest parts of our beings, sometimes triggered by unknown and long-submerged traumas. Emotions ebb and flow like the tide. They wash over the mind like rain in a thunderstorm. They are like our own inner weather. It can be difficult to weather the rain as such powerful forces downpour and assail your consciousness. The emotional realm is linked with feminine energy and the Goddess, as she holds dominion over the seas. When you are having difficulty managing your emotions, it can be very healing to meditate on the element of Water. Water can help you to learn to navigate your feelings, like a skilled captain sails the ocean.

Water is also a transformative element. It is able to occupy three distinct states of matter within temperature ranges that are detectable by humans. It is the only substance in the known universe that actually expands when it is cold, rather than shrinking. This allows ice to freeze on top of the water.

When heated, it forms into steam, increasing the humidity in the air. When it rises into the air and forms clouds, it takes part in the rain cycle—which is one of the main processes that make planet Earth habitable. It moves through many different processes and forms throughout its life, just as we do.

This element is deeply associated with cleansing and washing. Many religions include being submerged in water as a way to be reborn. Christianity has this rite in the form of baptism. Judaism has a ritual called the Mikveh. It is common in religions across the world. On a purely material level, humans use water to wash away the dirt and grime we accumulate as we go through our day to day lives. When this is translated into a spiritual level, water gains the power to wash away negative energies that attach to us as we move through life. When we are submerged, we are completely enclosed in the purifying liquid, and thus our whole being is cleansed.

Just as people are submerged in water in ritual, so too they are submerged in water for the first nine months of their life. The amniotic fluid of the womb is the generative waters in which we all begin life. It can be likened to the "primordial soup" out of which it is said that all life crawled. All life on Earth began in the seas. The very first lifeforms were microscopic microorganisms that evolved into ever more complex creatures until they became the vast array of life we know today. The water of the womb holds all of this potential.

Other bodily liquids are also associated with the element of Water—namely, sweat and tears. When we work our bodies very hard, we excrete sweat to cool ourselves and to regulate our body temperature. When we experience intense periods of emotion, we excrete tears from our eyes. Here Water holds yet another link to the emotional aspect of the self. Humans connect to overpowering emotions, whether joy or sorrow or anger, through our tears. When the tears begin to flow, we are physically manifesting the element that holds dominion over this aspect of our being.

# Chapter 4: Tools of the Trade

Now that we have discussed the history, deities, and the four elements, we can begin to discuss the sacred tools used within the Wiccan system. The four sacred tools outlined in this chapter each have a correspondence with one of the four elements. Thus, it is important to gain a working knowledge of Earth, Air, Fire, and Water prior to working with each of these four tools. Though there are four main tools that should be found on every Wiccan altar, there are a few other supportive tools that might be helpful for you to acquire. After reading this chapter, you should have a good understanding of what your ritual table should look like.

## Athame

Perhaps the most famous tool is the athame or ritual knife. This is a sacred tool that directs and moves energy. It should never be used to physically cut anything. This mixes it with mundane energy and makes less spiritually "sharp," or less able to direct the flow of your will. Altar objects are sacred, and should not be used for profane or mundane tasks such as cutting bread or snipping loose ends.

When it comes to the athame and the wand, some schools say that the athame is associated with the element of fire, and the wand is associated with the element of air. Going back to the days of the ancients, the Golden Dawn tradition, as well as the Rider-Waite tarot card decks both hold that the sword or dagger is associated with the element of Air. The phrase "the pen is mightier than the sword" comes to mind; both have to do with communication and are the domains of the element of Air.

Just as invoking the element of air in the magical circle calls in the mental aspect of the self, so too does placing the athame on the altar invoke the part of the self-called the mind. The sharp edge of the ceremonial dagger represents the logic we use to cut through the confusion, and how the sharp mind can discern truth from lies. When used in spell work, this tool is especially useful in situations where it is hard to discern what is true from what is false. The athame can be used to invoke the spirit of Truth, to clear the air and to dispel falsehoods. You can use this tool to call in clear sight, both physically and metaphorically to heighten powers of visual perception.

The athame is also the primary tool for directing and moving energy during rituals. Because of its long shape, when it is held in the hand, it acts as an extension of the arm. When you call down the energy, it runs down the length of the arm, and then down the length of the blade. The additional length gives greater precision in the movement and manipulation of energy. Some people direct energy using only their pointed fingers; however, this can be tricky for beginners, and newbies often find it easier to start out using a tool to direct energy. Once you have gotten the hang of directing the energy, you can start to use this tool to cast magical circles.

Aside from directing and moving energy, this tool is also excellent for symbolic rites of cutting and severing. Due to its sharp edge, it can be used to sever energetic ties. Just as a knife can cut threads, so too can the ceremonial knife cut spiritual threads. Sometimes we find ourselves connected to situations, places, or people that are harmful and cannot be repaired, and we wish to sever those connections, but do not know how. In spell work, the athame is an excellent tool to release the connections and bindings that are holding us back. When casting a magical circle, it is also important that the border remains intact and unadulterated. An athame can be used to cut a doorway in the sacred circle so that the ritual participant can enter and leave the circle without disturbing the boundary.

The ritual dagger also serves as a representation of the masculine half of the Divine Pairing, the God. There are two primary reasons for this. Firstly, it has a long and phallic shape, representative of God's sexual organ. The second reason it is associated with God is due to the dagger's associations with action, sharpness, defense, and warfare. God is the active part of the Divine Pairing, and placing the ceremonial dagger on the altar ensures that God is represented. In spell work, this aspect of the athame can be used to invoke the power of God, as well as his protection and strength. If you have something in your life that needs defending, then you can invoke God through the athame to ensure that it remains safe and sound. A ceremonial dagger is a dynamic tool with many uses.

## Chalice

The chalice is a glass, typically with a stem. It can look a bit like a wine glass and is typically made out of stone, metal, or glass. The chalice, like the athame, has a complex array of associations and functions and can be used in a variety of ways. There are the mundane functions that it serves, such as acting as a container for liquid, to the more esoteric, such as serving as the representation of the Goddess.

The chalice is closely associated with the element of water, as is expected of a vessel whose primary purpose is to hold liquid. Being indicative of the element of water, the chalice also holds within it the healing mysteries of this element. If you are performing spell work for healing (whether spiritual, emotional, or physical) you can use the chalice as a focal point for your work. If you are performing work in conjunction with the moon, the chalice should be your tool of choice, as it represents water, which is ruled by the moon. The moon rules lakes, oceans, and streams, as well as the watery elements present in the human body: blood, sweat, and tears.

Another vital function that the chalice serves is that it holds the sacred ale during sabbat rituals. The term "ale" is used loosely; it may refer to any consecrated liquid drunk in a ceremonial manner during the ritual. In Wiccan rites, it is common to pass cakes and ale. When passing the ale, which is contained in the chalice, participants state the phrase "may you never thirst." When passing the cakes, they say "may you never hunger." This is an act of blessing your fellow participants so that they will never know deprivation of the basic necessities of survival. The chalice is also representative of the "cup that runneth over," or the ale that never runs dry. It is a symbol of plenty, of the limitless ability of the Goddess to provide. You can use the chalice in spell work if you are experiencing times of lack and a shortage of basic necessities. It can help to bring times of plenty and abundance to your life.

Just as the athame is associated with God, the chalice is associated with the Goddess. An athame is a phallic tool, whereas this tool is representative of the sacred womb of the Divine Feminine. Placing the chalice on the altar ensures that there is a balance between the two elements of the Divine Pairing; this balance ensures smoother and more balanced spell work. This tool not only holds water but is representative of the water of the womb. It holds feminine energy that is open and receptive. Whereas the athame represents direct, focused action and the intentional movement of energy, the chalice draws in universal energy in a nonspecific, cumulative way. It gathers energy to the altar, and the other tools direct that energy.

This tool is also representative of the emotional aspect of the self. This is because emotions flow like water, or roll through like clouds. Water is emblematic of the movements of the unconscious mind, the subconscious self. Oftentimes we become emotionally wounded, whether due to being slighted, suffering heartbreak, or through neglect in our closest relationships. Though the wounds may not be physical, they can hurt just as badly as injuries to the flesh. The chalice is the most useful tool for spell work involving emotional healing. Due to the shape of the chalice, and its function of drawing in energy, it is an excellent tool to draw in the healing you may be searching for.

One way to draw healing into yourself is to consecrate water by placing it in the chalice. Once you have blessed it during the ritual, you can leave it to charge by the light of the moon (full moon is best). The moon is one of the physical manifestations of the Goddess, and by placing the water beneath her rays when she is brightest; you are imbuing it with her healing powers. Drinking the charged water is an excellent spell for healing. This tool should be placed on the western quadrant of the altar, as the element of Water is associated with this direction.

## Wand

The wand is perhaps one of the most mysterious tools on the Wiccan altar. It is also the magical tool that most lay people are familiar with. Anyone who has watched Harry Potter has seen the way that they wave wands around. Of course, the Wiccan wand will produce results, but none that are as flashy as a Hermione Granger saying *Wingardium leviosa.*

The wand's primary use is to move and direct energy, much like the athame. However, the wand is for use with spirits and energies that may be intimidated by the dagger and its steel blade. Some energy simply dislikes metal. Much like the athame, it has a phallic shape and can be used to represent God and anchor the masculine energy in a ritual or altar.

The wand's primary elemental association is with fire. Some more modern traditions use the wand to represent air and the athame to represent fire, but the Rider-Waite tarot system, which dates back to the 16th century, uses the wand to represent fire. Bowing to tradition, we will also do so here.

Fire is a powerful element and can be used for cleansing. If you find yourself in a situation where everything seems hopeless, or you desire personal transformation, the wand is an excellent tool. When used properly, you can invoke the energy of the Phoenix, and allow your life to undergo alchemical transmutation and burn away those things which no longer serve you. However, you should be careful with this tool, because fire can also burn you.

The wand and its associations of fire are also extremely useful in spell work calling for manifestation. Fire is raw power and can be used to generate the reality we inhabit. Or, in another perspective, fire can be used as the torch to guide the things you desire towards you. When performing spells to manifest certain things in your life, a common method is to hold the wand before you while imagining your desire coming towards you from the distance. Fire though, as previously stated, is a tricky element; this is a case of "be careful what you wish for," because there is a very good chance you will get it. Fire is raw power and is able to bring new realities into being.

The wand is also an expression of will. Will is innately linked with the element of fire. In the movies, someone waves a magic wand and then their desire is made manifest, whether that means moving an object or turning someone into a toad. In Wiccan spell work, using the wand to move energy involves using your will to manifest the desired reality. You may not be able to make a rabbit spontaneously appear, but you can draw those things to you that would enhance your prosperity and well-being. With the wand, you are able to bring forth your dreams into the world, much like alchemical salamanders are said to emerge from the flames. The inner desires become manifest in the outer world.

The wand also embodies energy and movement, as fire is. Fire is not just a chemical reaction between oxygen and flammable material. It is the dynamic energy of life itself. The electricity that causes the heart to beat, the energy that flows through the muscles and animates the brain, is all manifestations of fire, as represented by the wand. When you need to tap into a greater source of energy for your spell work, the wand is a great tool. It is emblematic of the power of the sun, the great fire in the sky that is the basis of all life. It is a ceaseless font of energy; it is always blazing, always moving, never at rest. If fire rests, it ceases to exist. Fire is the most mysterious state of matter, the plasma. Gas, liquid, and solids are all stable. Plasmas are constantly in flux.

Finally, fire represents the aspect of the self that is Spirit. It is the unseen force that animates the body, the most mysterious part of our embodiment as humans. One moment, a person is walking and talking. The next moment, their animating force has deserted them, and all that is left is an empty shell. The wand on the altar represents this most mysterious aspect of our being.

## Pentacle

The final tool that is commonly found on the Wiccan altar is the pentacle. It is representative of the element of Earth, and commonly takes the form of a small platform or dish that is placed upon the ritual table. The pentacle is also the symbol for the religion of Wicca. This five-pointed star enclosed in a circle has become culturally synonymous with witchcraft.

The pentacle in this sense is a small wooden or stone disc with a five-pointed star engraved upon it, enclosed within a circle. It is used in several ways. Firstly, it is a consecration tool. Due to the fact that it is engraved with the sacred symbol of Wicca, it blesses those things it comes into contact with. Sitting on the altar, the ritual table becomes a sacred space. Additionally, it blesses any items that are placed upon them. If you wish to consecrate crystals, pieces of jewelry, or other small items, they can be placed upon the pentacle during the ritual. Alternatively, they can be left on the pentacle over a period of time to charge.

Representing the element of Earth, the pentacle holds the energy of this element during rituals. The pentacle is linked with Earth's associations of spring, fertility, and growth. If you are feeling stunted in your life or inhibited in your efforts, you can use the pentacle to call on the element of Earth. In spell work, this can channel new growth, fertility, and prosperity into your endeavors. If you are experiencing a period of high anxiety, you can use the pentacle to help ground yourself in physical reality, and to soothe fear. If you are experiencing times of instability in matters of health, family, or home, the pentacle can be used to bring steadfastness, stability, and prosperity to these areas.

The pentacle is representative of worldly prosperity. It can be used in spells that are calling for material stability and well-being. A representative of Earth, it is emblematic of flowers blossoming, trees bearing fruit, and the bounty of the natural world. In the human world, when the Earth element is flowing freely it results in success in business, improved physical well-being, the health of the family, and all of one's basic needs being met or exceeded. However, using the pentacle to call material prosperity can be tricky. It is highly unlikely that performing a spell to buy a winning lottery ticket will make you the next millionaire. However, it can help you to ensure that you never want for the basic necessities of life.

The pentacle also performs an important job in terms of the magical and energetic circuitry being built upon the altar. The chalice receives energy, and the athame and wands directly that energy. The pentacle, though, grounds and stabilizes that energy. With deep roots that stretch deep into the ground, the element of Earth acts as a sort of ground on the lightning rod; it ensures that the correct amount of energy is flowing through the system at all times, and doesn't overload the magical work. It also serves as a bridge between the magical energy being summoned and physical reality. If the energy being called is unable to manifest in physical reality, then you might as well have not performed any spell work at all. The pentacle allows the spell work to manifest in the material world, and it also stabilizes the energy being called down.

Air represents the mind; Water represents the emotions; Fire represents the spirit; and finally, Earth represents the physical body. Placing the pentacle upon the altar allows us to recognize the corporeal aspect of our being. By placing all four tools (athame, wand, chalice, and pentacle) upon the altar, we recognize all aspects of our being. Through magical work with our altars, we are able to, through time; bring all of these different aspects of our being into harmony with each other. One aspect cannot exist without the others. The physical body is honored as the vessel that holds the spirit. The pentacle represents not only the Earth but how our bodies are manifestations of Earth. After all, the atoms that make up our body came from the Earth. The physical body allows the spirit and the mind to experience the world.

Each of these tools has a specific set of functions and associations. When used separately, they are helpful tools for tapping into and directing energy and performing spell work. When placed all together on an altar, they become a powerful array of magical circuitry to help you tap into the sacred.

# Chapter 5: The Wheel of the Year

Many people in the West view time as a linear construct. One month follows another, one year follows the next, and on and on from the beginning of time until the end. However, this is not the way that our ancestors interacted with time. Prior to the invention of the Gregorian or other linear calendars, our ancestors had a more cyclical understanding of the passage of time. They understood the flowing of one season to the next. Wiccans call this cyclical understanding "The Wheel of the Year." Wiccans understand that time is not a linear marching of days, but a turning of small and large cycles that wax and wane, and return again. Spring will come again, just as the dark moon will return to fullness. This chapter will explore the cyclical perspective of time that underlays the Wiccan understanding of the world; the next chapter will take a deep-dive into each of the eight Wiccan holidays. Learning to understand the flow and rhythms of the seasons will help you better taps into the magic of the natural world.

# Spring

In Western society, the term "springtime" refers to the very specific date: March 21st. This calendar date is derived from the vernal equinox or spring equinox. Not many people pay too much attention to this date nowadays, as they have lost touch with the turnings of the seasons. Most people will notice the days getting warmer and the snow receding, but few will notice the more nuanced changes that herald this time.

The early buds begin to swell and appear on the trees. The plants are shaking off the sleep of winter, and beginning to put energy into new growth. Soon not only are new leaves appearing but flowers as well. Pollen will soon start to irritate the allergies or those with sensitive noses. The early flowers are beginning to appear. First, the snowdrops push their white heads above the soil; they are the earliest. Then the daffodils begin to poke up; and finally, once the tulips begin to bloom, you know that spring is well and truly underway. The insects begin to awaken too; though mosquitoes aren't usually met with much joy, the bees are a welcome sight as they flit from flower to flower.

This time in the Wheel of the Year can be equated with the youngest part of the human life cycle, childhood. The young year is representative of the young person. Both are literally and metaphorically buzzing about with seemingly endless amounts of energy. There are a childlike innocence and curiosity to explore every new bud, every new flower, and to turn over every rock to see the newly-awoken worms wriggling beneath. The springtime is fresh and undisturbed by the trials and tribulations of the coming year. Children are still innocent and awestruck by the world and have not yet had their innocence taken by the harsh experiences of the world.

The first movements of the animal world are no doubt the birds. Everyone notices when the noisy geese start to fly north. It is a happy sign when the red-breasted robin is pecking for worms in the yard. Both the birds and the robins are busy building nests and laying eggs; and, in the case of the geese, angrily defending the aforementioned nest from any wayward wanderers. Other animals are bearing their young, too. Rabbits, foxes, deer, coyotes—all of these animals bring new life into the world with the start of the spring season. Just as the plant world is spreading its progeny with flowers, so too the animal world is spreading it's giving birth to the next generation.

For our ancestors, this was the time when they planned out what crops they would be planting for the year, and then put the seeds in the ground. The physical act of plowing the soil was backbreaking work, but it was necessary in order to ensure that they would have enough food later on that year. Taking each seed and deliberately placing it in the soil was not only a menial task but a metaphorical act of magic, in which our ancestors communed with the natural world and the possibilities of nature. Spring is an excellent time for you to meditate on the things that you would like to accomplish or manifest in the year; what metaphorical "seeds" do you want to plant for your life?

Spring is an excellent time to perform magic for prosperity, fertility, and growth. It is easy to tap into the growth-energy surging through then the natural world and apply it to your magic. If you are trying to start a new business, begin a family, or achieve new levels of prosperity in your life, spring is an excellent time. You can tap into the abundant energy of growth all around you to perform magic and rituals to accomplish your goals.

## Summer

For most people, summer begins Memorial Day weekend. On official government calendars, it begins on June 21st. For the ancients, however, summer began on May 1st, with the fire festival of Beltane. Summer was a favorite time of year in the ancient world because life was easy. There was hard work to be done in the fields, but the natural world was providing everything that they needed to survive. Berries were ripening, wild game was fattening up from the long winter, and new livestock was being born.

During this time, the deer are growing new antlers. You can see the velvety nubs on their heads growing slowly as the season progresses. The small animals have completely grown up; the rabbits have left the warren, and the songbirds have fledged and left the nests. The babies of the larger animals, such as deer, foxes, and wolves, have begun to enter adolescence and are learning how to survive from their mothers. The plants have shed their springtime flowers and are now sporting rich green leaves; many are also actively producing fruit or putting effort into doing so by the time that the autumn rolls around. It is a time of warmth, growth, learning, and maturing.

Summer is the part of the year that corresponds with young adulthood in the cycle of human life. The summer is the "prime" of the year; similarly, young adulthood is when we are in the "prime." The sun is at the height of its power and the Earth is at the height of its growth and prosperity. Similarly, humans during this phase have strong bodies that are able to accomplish many amazing feats, and they have amazing amounts of energy to go out and accomplish their dreams. This is one of the most energetic times of the year, with animals feasting in order to put on weight for the winter. Young adulthood is also one of the most energetic times of someone's life, as they go out in the world and attempt to figure out who they are.

During this time of year, there was an astounding amount of feasting that happened in ancient times. Because this was the season of plenty, there was no starvation, and the days were long. There was finally time to enjoy life. Even though there was a massive amount of work to be done intending the fields, once the day's work was done, our ancestors lit fires and took lovers down to the woods. This time of year was the height of work, but also the height of pleasure. The work largely consisted of weeding the fields, watering them to ensure the young plants grew to their full height and tending to livestock to ensure that the herds stayed strong, healthy, and well-fed.

If you are performing spell work in which you are trying to effect changes out in the physical world, summer is the best season in which to do it. In correspondence with the principles of yin and yang, winter is yin, or the still, quiet, and receptive season. Summer is the yang season: it is full of action, power, and movement. You can tap into that power to cause change. The sun is also at its fullest power on the summer solstice; you can tap into the powerful, manifesting power of the sun's fire, and use that energy in your spell work. Manifestation is associated with the element of fire; the summer is also associated with the element of fire. Use this fiery power to manifest those things in your life which you most need. However, it is also necessary to exercise extreme contemplation, restraint, and discernment when attempting to harness so much fiery energy. As previously stated, fire can burn. And in the case of manifesting your desires, be sure that you really want what you are attempting to summon to your life; after all, you just might get it.

## Fall

Today, most people associate autumn with apple cider and pumpkin spice lattes. When the leaves begin to fall, many people rush out to take photos of the many different colored tree leaves. For the ancients, though, fall was the beginning of a time of fear. The days were starting to shorten, and the looming shadow of winter appeared. Like squirrels, our ancestors furiously put away stores for the winter, knowing that the amount of food they put away would be the only thing standing between them and starvation.

The most noticeable thing that happens during this season is the changing of the leaves. The turn vibrant red, orange, or yellow, and begin to drop. There are more subtle signs too, though. The last of the fruits are beginning to ripen on the branch and on the vine. The days have reached equal length, and soon the nights will be longer than the days, signaling the descent into the dark season of winter. The behaviors of the animals have also begun to change. Those who will stay through the winter are fattening up in order to ensure they will have stores to make it through the cold season. Those that will not stay begin to migrate away. Everyone is familiar with the great V's of geese that begin to head south for the winter.

This part of the year is associated with middle age in the human life cycle. Just as the natural world has begun to lose the vibrancy and vigor of summer, so too do people at this age begin to lose the physical prowess and vibrancy of youth. The natural world is also putting out prodigious amounts of fruit and bounty. Similarly, people who have reached this age have begun to metaphorically harvest the lessons of their life and to turn their experiences into valuable wisdom and resources for their communities. While this season may not have the ease of summer, it is when the true work of one's life begins to bear fruit.

This time of year is excellent for spells to help you maintain stamina to the end of the finish line. If you are running low on energy and trying to complete a project or idea that you have long labored on, you can tap into the magic of this time of year in order to help your project bear fruit. You can also use the energy of the natural world to gain insight as to what you should be harvesting from your life. This time of year is an excellent opportunity to review the lessons of your life and metaphorically "harvest" the wisdom that you might find there.

## Winter

The modern day has robbed winter of the worst of its bite. People get cold, but they can retreat into heated houses, put hand-warmers inside their gloves, and get where they need to go inside of heated automobiles. It is only when the power goes out in the middle of a blizzard that people begin to feel a twinge of what our ancestors felt in the face of the coldest season. They huddled together around great hearths for warmth, carefully rationing out their stores, hoping that they would last until spring. With so many people so close together, illness and sickness spread easily during this time.

The natural world is blanketed in stillness. If you have ever wandered out in the middle of a snowstorm, you'll notice that the world is eerily quiet. It's as if the entire landscape has become hushed; there is no movement, and it is easy to believe that you are the only creature or person in the world. This season is the height of yin energy or stillness. It is the time for receptivity, for meditation and turning inward. All of the animals are hidden in their burrows hibernating or have flown south for the winter. There are very few animals that are active during this time. You may see the flash of fox hunting, or catch a glimpse of a squirrel digging up a cache of nuts it stored earlier that year. For the most part, though, all of the animals have gone to ground. The only thing that is still green is the pine trees. Their tough needles ensure that they can stay green even in the deepest cold. To our ancestors, those evergreen trees were symbols of the greenery that would return with the spring, which is why they brought sprigs of them inside.
This time of year equates with old age and death in the human life cycle. Just as the world has gone quiet and still, so too in old age do we slow down. The world enters into a meditative state, and old age provides us with the opportunity to reflect on the experiences of our lives. Just as our ancient ancestors gathered around hearth fires in the winter and told stories, so

too does old age provide us the opportunity to connect with our communities and share the wisdom that we have gathered over the course of our lives. In olden times, elders were venerated and held in high regard, because the wisdom that they held in their living memory was a valuable resource for those trying to figure out the best ways to live their lives.

This was the time of waiting for our ancestors. They would ration their stores and hope that the food they had put away would last until the spring thaw. It was a time when the fear of starvation was very real. Because people were so close together in such cramped quarters, people grew ill very easily. It was a hard time. However, it was also a time of storytelling and communal gathering. It was the time when the community came together from their scattered summer wanderings and duties and forged strong clan and tribal ties. It is these ties that united them as a people.

If you are lost and seeking wisdom in your life, winter is an excellent time to perform magic to seek the wisdom of your ancestors. It is also a great time to perform restorative magic. Winter is the meditative season. This season is a wonderful opportunity to gather energy in preparation for the work of the coming year.

# Chapter 6: Sabbats

In Wicca, sabbats are the celebrations that occur throughout the year, and which coincide with the changing of the seasons as well as the equinoxes. As a nature-based faith, Wiccan practitioners mark their days in conjunction with the natural world, recognizing and celebrating the ebb and flow of life in all things.

The sabbats also follow the mythical stories of the god and the goddess: at Yule, the Oak King (or Sun god) is born, and he grows quietly towards adolescence throughout the winter. At springtime, he and the goddess are young adults, joining together to bring life back to the Earth at Beltane, the sabbat observed on the first of May. At the height of summer, when Litha is celebrated, the Oak King has reached maturity, and soon after he declines, giving his body to the Earth at Lammas so that the harvest may be bountiful. At Litha/midsummer, the Holly King is born—a mirror opposite of the Oak King, and he grows to maturity until, at Yule and the darkest night, he succumbs to old age as well to nourish the sleeping animals and plants beneath the mantle of winter's snow and ice.

# Yule

Yule occurs on the winter solstice, between December 20th and 23rd. It is known as the shortest day of the year, as well as the darkest night, for those living in the Northern hemisphere.

At Samhain, we began to sense that the Veil—the wall between the living world and the spiritual world—was opening. Picture a curtain in a theater slowly becoming transparent, until it's gone. That's what's happening after the Oak King passes into the Earth at the end of summer, culminating at Yule. This is a time for reflection, remembrance, and most importantly—survival. When the Veil is gone, the gods and goddesses are busy, attending to their affairs. They haven't completely left humanity's side and you can still pray to them, but they are voices in the dark of winter, far away.

That is why at Yule; we gather close and celebrate community because the community is what enabled our ancestors to survive the cold, dark winter.

**The rebirth of the Sun.** On this night, the slow return of the sun is celebrated. Wiccans carry on the traditions of the ancestors when crops and trees were blessed with cider, called *was-*

*sail*, and wine and gifts of the harvest's fruits were given from house to house. In some countries, a tradition of giving books continues to this day. Rituals to cheer the spirit and keep the dark at bay, such as the lighting of candles and bonfires, are also practiced in modern times.

**Symbols of Yule.** Mistletoe, holly, the adorning of evergreen trees—thought to be aspects of the divine by Celtic peoples—are all originally pagan symbols and used to decorate homes and altars during this sabbat. Additionally, the **yule log** was used to celebrate the rebirth of the Sun god, using a small piece of last year's log to set this year's ablaze after it's been decorated with pine, blessed with wine or cider, and sprinkled with flour—the representation of the mingling of the god and goddess.

**Gods and Goddesses of Yule:** Any sun gods and mother goddesses, as well as triple goddesses. Fire goddesses such as Brigid.

**Herbs:** thistle, frankincense, rosemary, sage, laurel, bay.

**Foods:** wassail, liquor-soaked cakes, roasted game meats or pork, turkey, bread.

**Colors of Yule:** gold, green, silver, white, and red.

**Crystals:** Herkimer diamond, bloodstone, agate, pyrite, amber, emerald.

**Appropriate spell work:** Anything to do with love, friendship, rekindling, inspiration, warmth, and comfort. Yule is a good time to focus on the positive and reaffirm one's self.

# Imbolc

Also known as Candlemas and St. Brigid's Day, Imbolc is celebrated on February 2nd. It celebrates the first, inspirational spark that happens when we feel the hidden life beneath the frozen soil stir. The word "Imbolc" means "in the mother's belly", and so can we consider the sleeping seeds and hibernating animals at this time, in Earth's womb. Another name for this sabbat was Olneic, meaning "ewe's milk", dating back to traditional lambing season. On Imbolc, we celebrate the hope of life during the middle mark of winter.

The maiden goddess is celebrated at this time, and the sabbat is particularly auspicious of Brigid, the Celtic goddess of fire, poetry, blacksmithing, midwifery, and inspiration. The proper pronunciation of Brigid is the *bride*, and new brides and maidens are held in great regard on this day. Corn dollies and Brigid's crosses made of corn leaves are made to decorate the altar and give as gifts.

At this time of year, it's a good practice to symbolically sweep out last year's energy with a besom, in order to sweep in the new. Crocuses are a symbol of the maiden goddess, testing the air to see if spring is close by. Light a candle in each room to celebrate the goddess; go on walks in the snow to recognize and celebrate the first stirrings of spring.

**A time of inspiration and dedication.** This is a time when promises are made, devotions are set forth, and dedications to a new path are inscribed. New beginnings, reaffirmation of unions, and wiccanings (name-giving of children) are often celebrated and focused on.

**Symbols of Imbolc.** White flowers, candles, Brigid's crosses, copper, acorn-tipped wands to symbolize the sun god coming to adolescence, candle-crowns.

**Goddesses of Imbolc:** In addition to Brigid, this day is also the feast-day (birthday) of the Yoruban goddess Oya, who represents fire, lightning, the rainbow, the beloved dead, and the marketplace.

**Herbs:** violets, vervain, basil, angelica.

**Foods:** dairy, herbal tea, seeded cakes, roasted sunflower and pumpkin seeds, greens.

**Colors of Imbolc:** white, pale green, yellow, pink, red.

**Crystals:** white quartz, citrine, amethyst, garnet, onyx.

**Appropriate spell work:** Reunion, renewal, commitment, planting the seeds of tomorrow.

# Ostara – The Spring Equinox

The vernal equinox arrives between March 20$^{th}$ and 23$^{rd}$, and on Ostara, we celebrate the fertility of the goddess in mother form. The ancient symbols of the egg and the hare are connected to the goddess Eostre, from which the word estrogen is derived.

At this time, the Sun god has also reached sexual maturity and enters into holy marriage with the goddess. Altars are decorated with symbols of fertility, as well as a chalice and athame, to symbolize the physical union of god and goddess.

Mythically, in nine months, the mother goddess will give birth to the harvest itself as well as the Oak King at Yule, in December. At this time, we give thanks for what we can expect to come to fruition in our futures, and for the ongoing fertility of the Earth.

At this time of year, we can see greater evidence of spring, and decorate our altars and homes with dyed eggs (preferably with natural dyes such as beetroot, tea, thistle, and other plants), and symbols of the hare.

**A time of planting.** Seedlings can be started indoors now, and the seeds of future endeavors marked by spell work and dedication, also. Plan a magical herb garden, and spend time out of doors breathing in the scents of new life.

**Symbols of Ostara.** Eggs, hares, baby animals, plants and flowers, pregnant mothers.

**Gods and Goddesses of Ostara:** All mother goddesses and fertility gods. Also Artemis, goddess of the hunt, Pan, the sun god Lugh, and the Horned God.

**Herbs and flowers:** ginger, frankincense, copal, chamomile, chickweed, iris, daffodils.

**Foods:** similar to Imbolc: herbal tea, seeded cakes, leafy dishes and dishes with flowers. Dairy dishes.

**Colors of Ostara:** green, yellow, lavender, white.

**Crystals:** amethyst, jasper, bloodstone.

**Appropriate spell work:** Prosperity, fertility, creativity, new endeavors.

# Beltane

Celebrated either on the eve of April 30th or the day of May 1st, Beltane celebrates the union of the god and goddess as lovers and the death of winter. In high spring, hearts and minds focus on the coming summer, and easier days full of life and abundance. Beltane gets its name in part from Belinos, an ancient god of fire. Traditions of Beltane include community bonfires, feasts, and Maypoles. This is the second time of the year when the veil between the worlds is thin, and we may feel unrest and change unfurling within us, often giving way to vivid dreams.

Ancient practices allowed established married couples to leave their wedding bands at home for this night; younger people would camp in the woods and arrive home by the morning to participate in the Maypole dances. The morning of May 1st is especially magical for water spells: dew, rainwater, and river water collected at that time may be used for luck and fertility magic.

At this time of year, it's a good practice give yourself permission to enjoy life to the fullest—whichever way that means for you, as long as it does no harm. Realize that even the most docile, quiet creature is permitted to kick up its heels sometimes. You are doing nothing more but celebrating the joy of being alive, in the name of the god and goddess.

**A time of community.** Many Wiccan solitary practitioners choose to come out for Beltane, whether it's to join others in a potluck feast, sit by a roaring bonfire, or join together to perform a traditional Maypole dance. It is a happy, festive time for all ages.

**Symbols of Beltane.** White flowers, candles, Brigid's crosses, copper, acorn-tipped wands to symbolize the sun god coming to adolescence, candle-crowns.

**Gods and Goddesses of Beltane:** Bacchus, Cernunnos, Hera, Pan, Sheela-Na-Gig, Oshun, Yemaya, Corn Woman. In addition, the faerie and nature spirits can be connected to at this time.

**Herbs and flowers:** hyacinth, lilac, rose, basil, oregano, and cinquefoil.

**Foods:** almonds and nuts, apples, vanilla-flavored cakes, Meade, oysters, fresh greens.

**Colors of Beltane:** orange, red, white, spring green, purple.

**Crystals:** bloodstone, hematite, rubies, tiger's eye, amber.

**Appropriate spell work:** Fertility, abundance, money-related magic, love blessings.

## Litha

The summer solstice occurs between June 20th and June 22nd, and this is the longest day of the year. This marks the height of power of the god, and the Green Man—a Briton god of the forest and whose ivy-wreathed face is found in many ancient churches to this day—is in his glory. Midsummer Eve is auspiciously connected to the faerie realm, and dishes of milk and honey are set beneath oak trees for the fae folk, in appreciation for their hard work of wild animal husbandry and tending the plants and flowers of summer.

In the midst of summer's abundance and life, there is a deeper meaning to Litha: the Oak King is doing battle with the Holly King, who will return to Earth soon to rule the darkening days until Yule. There is a power struggle between life and death, darkness and light. This is a good time to resolve conflicts within yourself and do magical work seeking to incorporate our shadows (natural qualities of ourselves we might be uncomfortable with) and make peace within our spirits.

While harvest is not yet here, Litha is still a good time to take stock of the blessings in your life and be thankful for what you have. Use this time to focus on life's joys, and strive to be in the moment as you celebrate them.

**A time of sunlight and fertility.** Fertility not only pertains to having children. For the artist, entrepreneur, or anyone who works with their hands, fertility means promise, innate talents, and the power to take raw talent and be successful at one's vocation. Be thankful for the gifts you've been blessed with. Make pacts to work hard to bring them to their highest peak. Thank the Sun god for his life-giving warmth at this time. Re-dedicate yourself to the god and goddess.

**Symbols of Litha.** Horned animals, the oak tree, flowers, fresh water, the wand, and the crown.

**Gods and Goddesses of Litha:** Herne (a woodland god), Lugh, Pan, the Green Man, Amaterasu (a Japanese Shinto goddess of the sun), Hestia (goddess of the hearth).

**Herbs and Flowers:** goldenrod, honeysuckle, jasmine, sunflower, vervain, mug wort, oak, elder, lemon verbena.

**Foods:** sweet cakes, dandelion wine, meade, foraged foods, eggs, freshwater fish, oatcakes, cheeses, honey.

**Colors of Litha:** forest green, pink, yellow, brown.

**Crystals:** emerald, peridot, chrysoprase, agate, amber, opal.

**Appropriate spell work:** Conflict resolution, unity, abundance, gratitude.

## Lammas

Also known as Lughnasadh, Lammas is celebrated on August 1st and commemorates the death of the Oak King and the birth of the Holly King. Summer is dying and harvest has begun. The days will soon grow darker, but until then, we give thanks for the god's sacrifice; the Oak King gives his body to the Earth to ensure the harvest is bountiful enough for us to survive the winter.

Under the hot sun, plants brown and wither, releasing their seeds to the soil for next year. This is the link between the Oak King and the flora and fauna of the world.

Lammas in ancient times meant "loaf mass". It is traditional to give gifts of bread. Additionally, the craftsman god Lugh, also connected with the sun, bade us work hard and relish the fruits of our labors.

At this time of year, it's a good practice to take stock of what we have and to see how far we've come in our endeavors and goals. While winter is around the corner, right now the sun is hot, the tables are full, and so should our hearts be. Relish the beauty of the natural world and let it buoy your spirits.

**A time of abundance and honoring ancestors.** In modern times we often take for granted how easy it is to acquire food and nourishment. For our ancestors, this was the least idle time of year. A good harvest was crucial to survival. Pay homage to your ancestors, and perform healing magic on behalf of those in the world who still have to struggle for food. Donate to your local food pantries or volunteer at community kitchens.

**Symbols of Lammas.** White flowers, candles, Brigid's crosses, copper, acorn-tipped wands to symbolize the sun god coming to adolescence, candle-crowns.

**Gods of Lammas:** Lugh, sun gods, and the Holly King.

**Herbs and plants:** goldenrod, bloodroot, garlic, Queen Anne's lace, apple, wheat, bee balm, barley, mint, meadowsweet, thistle, nettle, rue.

**Foods:** dairy, herbal tea, seeded cakes, roasted sunflower and pumpkin seeds, greens.

**Colors of Lammas:** white, pale green, yellow, pink, red.

**Crystals:** white quartz, citrine, amethyst, garnet, onyx.

**Appropriate spell work:** Reunion, renewal, commitment, planting the seeds of tomorrow.

# Mabon

Mabon continues the harvest that began at Lammas. It is known as the second harvest and is a time to celebrate family, home, and hearth, as well as the fruits of our endeavors.

Mabon also begins the more somber of the sabbats, as this is the time that the goddess descends into the underworld, passing through the veil. The Earth begins to cool and the plants of the forest, farm, and field are withering. The forests begin to pay homage to the goddess by seeming to light themselves ablaze with color; a tribute from the god himself.

At this time of year, it's to focus on giving thanks for what you have. You may not be a gardener or a farmer, but you toil and put care into something—be it your career, your art, raising your children, caring for your pets, or simply living a peaceful, authentic life. Celebrate all of the days that led up to this one, in making you the person you are today.

**A time of thankfulness, and the celebration of elders.** Elders hold a special place in the Wiccan community. For everything they've shared with us—their wisdom, their hard work, their love—we elevate them and place importance on them during the Mabon feast. The goddess at this time in the year becomes the Crone, and her consort, the god, prepares himself for death and eventual rebirth. It is a quieting of the world as living things prepare for rest and to be reborn in spring.

**Symbols of Mabon.** Cornucopia, gourd rattles, corn and wheat, apples, pumpkins.

**Gods and Goddesses of Mabon:** Persephone and Hades, Snake Woman, Thor, Dionysus, Bacchus, Herne, the Muses, Loki.

**Herbs and plants:** copal, benzoin, frankincense, Solomon's seal, sage, milkweed, tobacco.

**Foods:** bread, vegetables harvested from the garden, roast meats, root vegetables, corn, apples, pomegranates.

**Colors of Mabon:** red, brown, orange, gold, white, and black.

**Crystals:** lapis, turquoise, yellow agate.

**Appropriate spell work:** rites of passage, family and connection, personal strength, abundance, removal of doubt.

# Samhain

Arguably the most auspicious of the pagan holidays, Samhain (pronounced *sow*-when), marks the end of the year and the opening of the veil between the mortal world and the spiritual world. We honor our beloved dead and look upon the wheel of the year, as well as time itself, recognizing that death is not the end, but another place on the wheel. Life continues, and dark and light are simply part of the natural order of things.

Other names for Samhain are All Hallow's (or simply Hallows), Shadow fest (in Italian *Strega* witchcraft), and the Day of the Dead.

This time of year, we honor the goddess as Crone and the aged god as dark lord and lady. Darkness is not evil—it is a part of the natural world. Winter's days are shorter and the nights' darkness longer; death precedes birth and birth to death, and so forth turns the Wheel of the Year and of time itself.

At this time of year, we look to the spirit world with great care and empathy. We set places at the table, known as a mute supper, for the beloved dead. Our ancestors buried apples along the side of the road, set plates of food out on the doorstep, and hollowed out turnips to place candles into light the way of the dead to warm fires and loving hearts.

**A time of reverence.** This time of year, we honor all who have passed before us, as well as the god and goddess for all of the life they've given us in the year. We look at our own growth, and make vows for change or for courage, vows for love and for peace. We gather with our loved ones and reach out to our beloved dead to let them know that they will never be forgotten.

**Symbols of Samhain.** Pomegranate, apple, iron, cauldrons, besoms, jack-o-lanterns.

**Gods and Goddesses of Samhain:** Hecate, Oya (she also rules the cemetery), Isis, Baba Yaga, Rhiannon, the Morrigan, Lilith, Cerridwen, Kali, Hel, Ishtar. Hades, Ogun (Yoruban god of the forest and the forge), Anubis, Osiris, Cernunnos, Dionysus.

**Herbs:** mug wort, allspice, Mandrake, broom, sage, myrrh.

**Foods:** turnips, pumpkin, dark greens, baked bread, red wine, beef and pork, poultry, sweet cakes, and candies.

**Colors of Samhain:** orange and red, black, white, gold, and silver.

**Crystals:** jet, obsidian, onyx, iron, tiger's eye, white quartz.

# Chapter 7: Esbats

## What Is Moon Magic?

Humans have worshipped the moon and the sun for as long as there have been humans on Earth. Sometimes the moon is considered a male force of nature, and as such, the waxing moon is connected to the horned god, the full moon linked with the Fatherly aspect of the god, and the waning moon considered the elder god and the teacher.

More often, the moon is considered a planetary body that exists within the goddess's domain. The human menstrual cycle is typically 28 to 30 days, and so is the lunar cycle—the time it takes for the moon to travel around our Earth. The full moon is considered to be the fertile, motherly goddess, the waxing moon the maiden, and the waning moon the wise Crone.

Additionally, each full moon that occurs within a year—twelve to thirteen occurrences—has a name or special significance in many of the world's cultures, such as the native tribes of the Americas and Canada, the Irish people, and West African tribes.

When two full moons fall in the same month, the second full moon is known as a *blue moon*, and special celebrations and magic may be performed during this time.

**The shifting moon.** The phases of the moon and the corresponding full moons will always shift slightly against the solar calendar. This coincides beautifully with the nature of the moon itself—in magic and in Wicca, the moon represents deep mysteries and ancient wisdom, and the fact that not everything in life is obvious or easy to come by. The moon takes patience and a serene mind to understand, and it takes time. The moon teaches us that life is a lesson—so it's useless to rush certain things when only time will bring them to us.

**The cleansing and rejuvenating power of the moon.** Something pagans often do is lay out there magical tools and crystals to recharge beneath the light of the full moon (even if that full moon reaches peak fullness during the middle of the day). The moon's energy washes us in potent power, full of promise and fertility. The triple goddess has been worshipped for thousands of years, in many different cultures, and has always been linked to the three phases of the moon.

**The moon and the phases of life.** For everything, there is a purpose and a meaning. As the moon shifts from crescent, to full, to opposite crescent, so do we focus our magical work on the moon's phase at the time.

## The New Moon Esbat

The word *esbat* comes from the same Greek origins as the word *estru* and means monthly". Some covens and communities choose to have their monthly esbat during the new moon. This moon can be a time to work with either the maiden goddess or the crone. It is a time of dark energy—and again, dark in pagan faiths does not mean evil, it simply means of the darkness. The night is dark and so is the womb. Onyx and crow's feathers are dark, and so is the soil. So don't fear the dark! It is a time of potency—consider it a blank canvas.

During a new moon esbat, the altar can be decorated with things reflecting the new moon's energy:

- Items that represent the maiden such as flower buds and seeds, a cup of soil, moonstones, crystal, a silver cord, a crow's feather; items that represent the crone such as a bundle of dried herbs (rosemary is perfect for this), a cup of sand or ashes, black coffee, onyx, turquoise, or beryl, an owl's feather.

- A statue or painting of either the maiden or the crone.

- Brown, dark purple, dark red or black candles.

- A besom, or sacred broom, to sweep away negative energy.

- The usual magical tools: chalice, athame, wand, and pentacle.

- An offering for the goddess, such as a cup of fresh water, bread, candied ginger, white wine, or grape juice. Typically, one beverage and one food are given. These can be passed around the circle for each to take a small part of before offering it to the goddess, and the person passing this to each member will say as they do so, "Never hunger, never thirst." This blesses each for the coming month.

During a new moon esbat, one may focus on cleansing a space or one's self of negative energies. Esbats can be celebrated alone or within a group. If solitary, a ritual cleansing bath, smudging (using sage, rosemary, or palo santo to burn cleansing smoke) a house or living area, or lighting a black candle followed by a white candle are all effective, simple cleansing techniques. Writing something you want to be rid of, such as a habit, guilt, grief, or shame, can be written on a piece of paper and burned in honor of the moon.

Once the cleansing is complete, a blessing should follow. Always follow the bitter with the sweet. Light sweet incense, draw the power of the potent moon's potential into your space, and shake bouquets of sweet flowers with holy water or rainwater around the circle and on the altar. Ask the goddess to bless the coming days of the month with sweetness and joy.

Once all ritual is complete, thank the goddess or god for joining your circle and celebrate with the traditional pagan "cakes and ale". This can be any combination of food and drink and doesn't have to include alcoholic beverages.

## The Waxing Moon Esbat

During a waxing moon esbat, the altar can be decorated in such a way as to honor the maiden.

- Items that represent the maiden, such as fresh milk, spring or rainwater, new flowers, white quartz, found bird feathers, nuts and seeds, ceramic statues of birds or young animals, citrine, peridot, moonstones, and tiger's eye.

- A statue or painting of maiden.

- White, silver, gray, or pale green or pale brown candles.

- The usual magical tools: chalice, athame, wand, and pentacle.

- An offering for the goddess, such as a cup of fresh water, honeyed cakes, crackers or cookies, white sparkling grape juice or white wine.

During a waxing moon esbat, spell work and rituals involving beginnings, courage, and hope, starting a project, new love, and life's milestones may be conducted.

During the waxing moon, we can focus our meditations and magical work on things we want to see come to fruition. Projects we are beginning, or have been working on, hopes of fertility, new relationships, and a new goal— all of these are well-suited to focus on during the waxing moon. They can be simple, one-time spells, or spells that we return to each night or day leading up to the full moon.

# The Full Moon Esbat

During a full moon esbat, the altar can be decorated in such a way as to honor the mother goddess or horned god.

- Items that represent the mother goddess, such as seashells, gourds, fresh flowers, eggs, cups of soil with seeds planted in them, honey, sweet cakes, meade, fruity wine, white grape juice, fresh water; items that represent the horned god, such as animal horns or skulls, crow feathers, a sword, a wooden staff, a crown, a cup made of stone or wood, whiskey, amber ale, red wine or grape juice.

- A statue or painting of either the horned god or the mother goddess (or both).

- Green, red, violet, gold, yellow or blue candles.

- The usual magical tools: chalice, athame, wand, and pentacle.

- An offering for the god or goddess, such as a cup of fresh water, bread, sweet cakes or cookies, sparkling wine or grape juice.

During a full moon esbat, one can focus on manifestation, abundance, self-love and readying oneself for love, life goals and dreams, healing, and spells to encourage strength and courage.

A full moon esbat is a wonderful time to raise magical vibrations that help the entire community, as well as the world. If you or your coven know of an area that has been affected by disaster or tragedy, sending healing and recovery energy their way during a full moon is a worthy practice.

During the full moon, we may focus on anything that needs the utmost energy. It can be things we wish to reach culmination (or release, such as finally getting good feedback on a project or hearing back from a job we applied for); it can be a simple matter of rejuvenating our inner selves after a difficult month, or sending healing energy to ourselves or others. The full moon is a time for recharging, so we set our tools and sacred objects out in the moon's light (or windowsill if you won't have access to a private space outdoors). Potions and elixirs we've created can be charged now, as well as amulets, sachets, and candles.

**There is actually no "wrong" time for magic.** Magic for pagans, including Wiccans, is merely a tool to help us focus our energy. If there is a need for magical work, don't let the phase of the moon deter you—it will simply result in the effects of your magic manifesting in a different way. A protection spell during a full moon may make the spell caster stronger, and less likely to feel the effects of who or what they're protecting themselves from; a protection spell during a waning moon will more likely push the source of the attack away or decrease the attack's potency.

A job search spell cast during a waning moon might actually cause you to *lose* your current job, but successfully find a new one during the coming days because you have more time to look. It's all a matter of perspective.

## Waning Moon

During a waning moon esbat, the altar can be decorated in such a way as to honor the crone.

- Items that represent the crone goddess. Keep in mind that the crone actually embodies all three aspects of the goddess, as she's lived through all three phases! Symbols of the triple goddess and triple moon can be placed on the altar, as well as the waning crescent moon, images in the colors of the sunset, midnight blue stones and artifacts, statues of owls, black cats, ravens, smoking pipes, copal incense, bundles of dried flowers and herbs, fruit cakes, meade, cider, port, black tea or coffee with sugar, fresh water, rice, and dried fruits.

- A statue or painting of either the crone goddess.

- Black, brown, dark red, midnight blue, silver, gray, or dark purple candles.

- The usual magical tools: chalice, athame, wand, and pentacle.

- An offering for the goddess, such as a cup of fresh water, bread, fruit cake, ale or cider, or sparkling grape juice.

The waning moon is quite important, also, and never to be thought of as negative. Sometimes, things need to wind down and to be let go of. The plants and flowers wilting and dying at the beginning of autumn feed the soil, and so does letting go of things which no longer serve us. During the waning moon, we can focus on the magic that releases anything in our lives that we need to let go of. It's a great time to do protection magic, as well as magic that supports getting rid of bad habits, weight loss, or the burden of shame, guilt, or any other negative emotion that is holding us back from happiness. The crone's wisdom at this time is like a loving great grandmother's—she wants us to succeed and to be joyful, so allow her to help you make your life so. During a waning moon esbat, spell work and rituals involving banishing and protection may be undertaken, as well as bidding goodbye to something or someone, and helping those in mourning deal with grief. It is a good time of the month for a memorial ceremony.

The waning moon is quite important and never to be thought of as negative. Sometimes, things need to wind down and to be let go of. The plants and flowers wilting and dying at the beginning of autumn feed the soil, and so does letting go of things which no longer serve us. During the waning moon, we can focus on the magic that releases anything in our lives that we need to let go of. It's a great time to do protection magic, as well as magic that supports getting rid of bad habits, weight loss, or the burden of shame, guilt, or any other negative emotion that is holding us back from happiness. The crone's wisdom at this time is like a loving great grandmother's—she wants us to succeed and to be joyful, so allow her to help you make your life so.

## The Dark Moon Esbat

This moon is also referred to as "the dead moon". It is a brief period of time when the moon is completely dark, showing that face to us on Earth while fully facing the sun. The dark moon is a good time for inner work and self-reflection, and so lends itself more to solitary observance than to a group or community magic.

Magic does not always have to be used to create a reaction—magic is the action, and the results of that magic can be considered the "reaction". There are times when sitting in a magic-filled space and contemplating the path ahead can be healing and affirming: the dark moon is one of the best times for this.

During a waning moon esbat, the altar can be decorated in such a way as to honor the crone or the elder god.

- Items that represent the crone, such as smoked teas, chicory coffee, grape juice or red wine, honey cakes or panettone, wreaths of ivy, hematite stones or smoky quartz; items that represent the elder god, such as mahogany, driftwood, pipe tobacco, dark ale, dark fruits or vegetables such as plums or purple peppers, petrified wood, amber, or granite.

- A statue or painting of either the elder god or the crone.

- Brown, gray, silver, or black candles.

- The usual magical tools: chalice, athame, wand, and pentacle.

- An offering for the god or goddess, such as a cup of fresh water, bread, seeded crackers, licorice or herbal candy, dark ale, grape juice, red wine.

Magic suitable for this esbat includes drawing love to you, as well as healing old wounds, overcoming obstacles, protection against theft and those who would stalk us, navigating divorce or separation, and help with addictions or injuries. The dark moon is a potent time for any divination, be it through the use of tarot cards, crystal ball or water scrying, runes, or simple candle magic.

## The Blue Moon Esbat

The blue moon occurs when two full moons happen in the same month. Blue moon energy is thought to be even more potent than full moon energy.

The folklore surrounding the blue moon tends to focus on luck and blessings:

- If you turn a coin in your pocket during this time, you gain tremendous luck and good fortune.

- gather plants beneath a blue moon for use in abundance and fortune spells

- Charge and bless objects to be used in magical work for finding a new job, bettering your finances, legal matters, and travel on your altar or outdoors beneath the lucky blue moon's light.

During the blue moon, the altar may be decorated to honor the god and the goddess in the aspect you feel most drawn to.

- Items that representing the masculine and the feminine of the natural world, hopes, dreams, luck, and good fortune may be placed there: rainbow items or stones, clover, crocus, basil and oregano, fresh flowers, crystal and pyrite, coins and paper money of each denomination, gold and silver, seashells and snail shells, rain and storm water, honey, champagne, cognac, cigars, fresh soil with seeds planted, amethyst, emeralds, and onyx. Blue flowers such as violet, iris, hydrangea, borage, and purple roses are also an excellent choice.

- A statue or painting of either the god and goddess or both.

- Candles in your favorite color, or a rainbow of colors. You may also choose to decorate the altar with blue items and use blue candles.

- The usual magical tools: chalice, athame, wand, and pentacle.

- An offering for the god or goddess, or both. A good choice is to have a potluck and fix one or two plates of the food served. Have additional bread, crackers, cookies, and either grape juice, water, or wine to pass around.

Magic suitable for this esbat include inciting change, growth, and healing, as well as love magic, financial spell work, money luck, and gambling luck, improved health and well-being.

**Purifying during a blue moon.** As a community or as a solitary practitioner, the blue moon presents a perfect opportunity for cleansing one's self spiritually. One might start by standing beneath the moon itself if the weather permits, allowing the healing energy to cast away any negativity or spiritual decay that's gathered on you from the previous month. Then return to the altar, cast your circle, and call down the energies of the moon. Music may be employed to set the mood. Take a bundle of healing herbs and ceremoniously trace them over the body—from head to feet—then burn them in a cauldron or bonfire to release the negativity.

**Make a list of goals for the future.** Take time during the blue moon to focus on your hopes and dreams for the coming months, and ask the goddess to grant you the insight, energy, and power to make those dreams come true. Make a note of this in your book of shadows so you can reflect on it in the coming months.

# Chapter 8: Magic and the Book of Shadows

## What Is Magic?

Magic, to pagans, is very real. There are many misconceptions about magic, however. The magic that Wiccans practice is not evil, not so-called "black" magic—it is simply a tool to help achieve a result. Just as prayer, meditation, exercise, and therapy are all tools to change one's path and one's thinking, so does magic work to help one navigate more successfully through life.

There are many different types of spells that can be performed, using a variety of materials. Before you get started on your first magic spell, however, it's important to do some research.

**The timing of spells.** As we discussed in the previous chapter, the phase of the moon is important, but also negotiable. It's best to time your spell work with the appropriate moonphase, but if time is of the essence and the spell must be performed right away, then it can be done when you need to.

**Days of the week.** The days of the week also have magical significance. **Monday** is the day of the Moon, and good for beginnings, self-reflection, and healing. It is a mysterious day to work magic, so matters that are cut and dry are better left to other, more decisive days.

**Tuesday is a powerful day** and can lend itself well to matters of protection, finance, personal strength, and settling disputes in one's favor. Take care not to let your passions go to your head on this day, and strive to be peaceful in your affairs.

**Wednesday** is a good day for magic involving communication, career, getting the answers you've been waiting for, and expediting good news. Pray to the god Mercury, or to Ellegua—the trickster-messenger god of the Yoruba tribe—for aid in your work. Light incense and burn candles for Mercury to come swiftly. Offer Ellegua candies, cola, or a cigar for his help. Wearing red on Wednesday will bring good luck.

**Thursday** is a day ruled by Jupiter. It's a great day for spells regarding luck, prosperity, abundance, and beneficial change. Offerings of wine, purple fruits and cakes to Jupiter with incense will help the god come around to your aid.

**Friday** is a day important in love and business. Many gods and goddesses call this day their own, such as Freya (after which the day is named), Oshun, Oya, Venus, and Erzulie. Spells for romantic matters, magical work to influence customers in the marketplace, and spells to be successful in court are all good things to focus on.

**Saturday** is ruled by Saturn, though it is also connected to Oshun the African love and riches goddess as well. Spells of protection, cleansing, personal strength, and wealth can be performed on this day.

**Sunday** is, of course, the day of the sun, and magic pertaining to vitality, good fortune, love, wealth, new beginnings can be performed on this day.

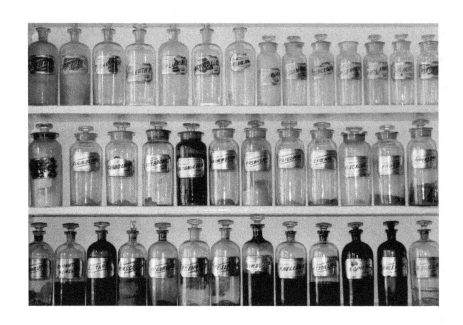

# Spell Components and the Magical Properties of Things

Now that you've selected the moon phase and day to perform your spell, what sort of things should you gather? A spell doesn't have to be complex unless you want it to be. Simple candle magic is incredibly effective, but so is herbal sachets and baths, herbal oils, and jar spells. Here are two lists to help you get started.

## *The magical significance of colors:*

- Blue: peace, healing, the mother goddess (such as Aphrodite or Yemaya), tranquility, wisdom. Use in spells for a peaceful home, fertility, and wisdom. Also good for helping one's psychic ability and communicating with angels.

- Green: fertility, growth, money magic, restorative magic, new beginnings, abundance. Use in spells for employment, good fortune, fertility.

- Yellow: communication, sexuality, attraction, intellectual matters, connection, magnetism. Use in spells for confidence, joyful sexuality, fertility, successful studies and high grades on tests, and communication.

- Orange: success, playful love, vitality, rejuvenation, energy. Use in spells for help with change, to enhance beauty and charisma, for success in one's craft, for confidence. Also a very good color for healing magic.

- Red: courage, strength in adversity, passionate love, health. Use in love spells, magic involving the power of will, and to enhance physical vitality.

- White: peace, mental balance, illumination, connection to ancestors, connection to the spirit world, blessing energy. Use to bless a space or a person, for a new home, to cleanse the spirit and body of negative energy, and for personal clarity.

- Black: protection, mysteries, banishing, binding, the wisdom of elders, fertility, stability. Use in spells for protection, banishing, transformation, and connecting to the elder god and crone goddess.

- Silver: psychic abilities, memory, clarity. Use for magic involving clairvoyance, creating a shield against negative energy, and spiritual awakening.

- Gold: the Sun god, past lives, intuitive powers, prosperity, new jobs, wealth. Use for money magic spells, spells for good luck, magic to connect to past life memories, and success.

- Brown: grounding energy, the Earth, fertility for the masculine, endurance, humble power. Use in magic for confidence, fertility, long-term financial success, a happy home, and for pets and other animals.

- Gray: self-reflection, neutrality, invisibility from one's enemies. Use in protection spells, neutralizing negative forces, understanding between two parties.

- Purple: wealth, luck, a rich life, delight, psychic powers, clairvoyant dreams. Use in spells to increase psychic ability, for good fortune, money magic, spiritual growth, connecting to angels and spirit guides, and self-control.

- Pink: romantic love, affection, youthfulness. Use in magic to remind oneself to find the beauty in things, for new romantic beginnings, magic for children.

## *The magical significance of popular herbs and flowers:*

- Acacia: protection, money magic, meditation, use in anointing candles and other magical objects. Also known as gum Arabic.

- Acorn: money magic, a happy home, amulets to promote youthful beauty, the wisdom of the elders and protection. Useful in luck magic.

- African violet: protection magic, lucky if kept in the home, good for the altar during Imbolc and Beltane.

- Apple: place on the altar during Samhain. Love spells, friendship, abundance.

- Basil: love, masculine energy, wealth, strength. Use in spells for a new job, success in business, and prosperity, as well as in love spells.

- Bay leaf: A super charge spells, luck, prosperity, protection, wishes coming true. Write a wish on a bay leaf and toss it in a fire to release your desire to the universe.

- Bayberry: good fortune, healing. Bayberry candles are excellent for money magic and to heal the heart.

- Carnation: spells of protection, inner strength, enhancing one's power in magic, ritual baths.

- Catnip: grown in one's garden or hung dried near the door, catnip protects the home.

- Cilantro: brings happy days to gardeners. Grown in the garden it will bring peace to the home.

- Cinnamon: luck, money, and passion. Use in spells to "heat up" the magic and expedite the results.

- Dandelion: divination, dreams, connecting to the spirit world. Use in sachets to help dreams come to fruition.

- Dragon's Blood: protection, cleansing. Burn to increase the potency of magical work. Carry for good luck.

- Echinacea: power, money, offerings to the spirits. Add to spells to boost their efficacy.

- Foxglove (poisonous to people and pets): beloved of fairies, protects the home as well as the garden. Grants visions.

- Frankincense: purification, noble endeavors, blessings.

- Garlic: protects the home and purifies spaces.

- Holly: joy in marriage, heightens masculinity, luck.

- Ivy: fertility magic, healing, protection against enemies.

- Job's tears: wishes comes true, blessings. Use in employment spells, mojo bags.

- Lavender: love, protection, peaceful heart. Helps with magical work to heal depression.

- Marjoram: purification magic, cleansing of spaces and self, used in sachets to attract wealth.

- Mint: helps businesses attract customers. Carry leaf in the wallet to ensure a constant flow of money in. Protects the home.

- Nutmeg: prosperity, money magic, luck. Use to break hexes.

- Oak: the tree regarded as most sacred. Use in fertility magic. Strength, wisdom, luck, vitality.

- Orange Blossoms: attraction, luck, money spells.
- Palo Santo: use to rid one's self and home from negative influences.

- Patchouli: love, money magic, luck.

- Rose: romantic and divine love, healing, avoiding negativity.

- Rosemary: sacred to faeries, ward against negativity, powerful banishing herb, and put in spells to boost power.

- Sage: traditionally used to cleanse a space. Also promotes healing, wisdom, and help with grief and mourning.

- Thyme: boosts reputation, hang in the home for protection and health.

- Vanilla bean: love and lust, increase magical abilities.

- Walnut: connection to the divine, blessings of the god and goddess, granting wishes.

## Preparing To Cast a Spell

Before you begin your magical work, make sure you prepare your space and yourself. You should have all of your ingredients and tools on hand. If you don't have a dedicated altar, a space on the floor that will be undisturbed by other people or pets will work fine. If you have time to take a ritual bath, that's great, but it's not essential.

When you're ready to begin, face the north. If you're unsure of where north is and do not have a compass, consider downloading a compass app for your phone, or look at an online map or surveyor's map of your property. You could also make note of where the sun rises and map the directions as such.

**Call the corners, or directions, to make your circle.**
You need a magical space that's filled with energy. You can't fill the entire world with your energy, so a circle gives you a dedicated space to work with. Start by facing north and saying Hail guardians of the north, I call to you in perfect love and trust." Then do so for each direction, turning clockwise (known as *sunwise* to Wiccans). Once you are done, say, the circle is cast." You are ready to begin your work.

# A Simple Candle Spell

Select a candle in the appropriate color, and anoint it with oil in an appropriate herb or herbal mixture. Set this on your altar or temporary magical workspace, and light it. Light a stick of incense, and select a candle in the appropriate color, and anoint it with oil in an appropriate herb or herbal mixture. Set this on your altar or temporary magical workspace, and light it. Light a stick of incense, and draw sunwise circles in smoke around the candle as it burns. State what you would like to come true when the spell is complete; be specific. Imagine these things coming true like scenes in your mind. When you are ready, set the incense in a holder, and say, "I create this magic, to do as I say, to work for me both night and day. I create this magic by three times three, to harm no one else nor bring harm to me. I create this magic, so mote it be." Allow the candle to burn down to its finish. Never leave a candle unattended, but safe places for it to burn include a metal sink, metal pot or cauldron, or the bathtub. Make sure pets and small children will not have access to it.

## Full Moon Abundance Spell

This spell requires the power of the full moon; other moon phases will not be strong enough for the work to be successful. Gather a coin of every denomination; add to this a silver dollar, and a golden dollar. Fill a bowl, cauldron, or cup with rainwater and set it on your altar or magical workspace. Light two candles—use colors that represent the sun and the moon to you, and set them on either side of the container you are using.

Drop one coin into the water at a time, saying, Night and day, sun and moon, abundance coming to me soon, never stop, these coins I drop, night and day, sun and moon."

Set your container of water with the coins to bask in the full moon's light. The next day, set the coins on your altar, or gathers them in a cloth bag to a place near your workspace, wallet, or computer.

## One or the Other Candle Spell

If you have a question or two things you need to make a choice from, pick a candle in a color appropriate to your concern, and make sure it is not a dripless" candle. Set it on a dish, and place a nickel on one side of the candle, a penny on the other. Designate which coin represents which choice; if this is a simple yes or no question then the penny is yes and the nickel is no. Anoint the candle in rosemary, lavender, or simply olive oil and light it, focusing your mind on the choices in front of you. Speak your question, and ask the god and goddess to allow the candle to answer it for you.

Let the candle burn out until it's finished, and examine which coin has attracted the most wax: that is your answer.

# Protection Spell for the Home

This can also be considered a spiritual cleansing" spell. Just like our carpets and our floors, our homes can get a lot of tracked in spiritual dirt", over time. After guests' visits or a repair person has come to fix the sink or just the simple act of you and your family coming home day after day, bringing with you the residual negativity of the outside world, it eventually will become necessary to sweep out the clutter so your unique, positive energy can shine through.

You'll want to gather four mason jars with lids that shut tight, some rice, lavender, and basil, as well as kosher salt for this spell.

**A note on spiritual cleansing.** Whether it's yourself, your house, a magical tool, or a piece of antique jewelry you found in a thrift store, mundane cleansing should always come before spiritual. Before you take a ritual bath, take a regular shower. Before you bless that vintage silver ring, polish it. Before you smudge your house, sweep it up, wipe the counters, and vacuum the rug. Doing this the day before sets your mind at ease so you can focus on your magical work.

Fill each jar with a handful of each ingredient. If you have a yard or outside space where neighbors won't pry, you can set each jar beside your house on each side, going from north to south. If you live in an apartment or flat or do not have private outside space, you can set a jar in a room that corresponds to each direction, at an exterior wall or on a windowsill.

As you set each jar down, say, North, south, east, and west, I ask you goddess, this house to bless." Let the jars remain a month and a day, then release the ingredients (toss in the garbage, in compost, or into the fire.)

# Spells to Open Yourself to Love

**Love spells** are possibly the most common spells desired, aside from money spells.

You can find countless love spells promising to win someone's heart, rekindle cooled affections, trick someone into falling in love with you, sweeping someone off their feet, etc. What is the intention here? You might say, "to gain love".

What is the only foundation for true love? It's trust.

Recall the Wiccan tenet that we say in a circle and in performing spell work: "In perfect love and perfect trust." Love that is tricked into being will never be perfect or true. Love that is not based on trust is doomed to fail or fail again.

If you feel that you are ready to open yourself to a new romance, there is absolutely no reason not to do a magic spell to help you along with that. Consider it a pact with yourself to begin to be the loving, nurturing person you can be—and to also be willing to accept love from others.

These are just a few items that are useful in a love spell: rose petals, oil, or incense; rose quartz, hematite, amethyst, patchouli, rosemary, hibiscus, river stones (ask permission from the river goddess and spirits before taking one, and leave a gift of fruit or flowers at the riverbank), and Adam and Eve root (orchid root).

For roses, generally yellow petals mean friendship and platonic love, pink means new romantic love, and red means passionate love.

**A simple love spell is to cut halves of one red rose and one white rose,** tie them to make a single flower with string, then toss this charm into the water of a river, lake or waterfall, asking for love to come to you.

**Use rose oil** to anoint a white, pink, or red candle, and write the qualities of love you desire in a relationship. Fold the paper towards you three times and let the candle burn down upon it.

**Write down the qualities you seek in a romantic partner**, fold the paper towards you three times and bind with red string, then pin inside a red cloth. Keep this charm on you to attract the attention of new, true love.

**Carry a sprig of goldenrod** in your pocket to attract a love that will be both rejuvenating and secret (at first). Goldenrod is actually not a cause of allergies as many thinks, as its pollen does not become airborne.

**Take a ritual bath** in rose petals, a drop of patchouli oil, and set rose quartz in the water with you. Close your eyes and imagine a moment together with your true love. Repeat the words, God and goddess, them and me, at this moment, I will cry. In perfect love and perfect trust, allow destiny to join us." Allow the bathwater to drain but save a cup of it, along with the rose petals. Pat yourself dry gently, allowing the residual bathwater to remain on your skin. Toss the cup of water with petals in a crossroads, and true love will come your way in three months' time.

**Tell your secrets to the river goddess.** Place the river stone you found on your altar. Write down your hopes and dreams about love. Write down good qualities you find in yourself, and also challenges you've overcome and bad habits you've been able to put aside. Tell the goddess that you are ready for love to come into your life. Fold the paper three times towards you and place it beside the stone. Whenever you need a reminder that you are ready, gently hold the cool, smooth stone to your heart, and say, "Loving goddess, I am ready for the love that awaits me," as an affirmation.

## Honey Jars

**Rootwork** is a combination of many traditions and magical practices, coming over from Africa and the slave trade. Slaves in America needed to hide their magical work to avoid punishment, and began the tradition of using magic to survive in situations that were often dire. Today, rootwork exists as folk magic, and its nature is to be able to use what's on hand to produce extraordinary results. For a money, wealth, or abundance spell, write your very specific wishes on a piece of paper with a pencil, taking care not to lift the pencil off the paper until the statement is complete, fold it towards yourself twice, and place it in the jar with wealth-drawing herbs, shiny things of gold or silver, such as coins, gems, or biodegradable glitter. Seal the jar and burn gold, green, or silver candle on top for seven days, then three days during each full moon.

## Full Moon Abundance Spell

This spell requires the power of the full moon; other moon phases will not be strong enough for the work to be successful. Gather a coin of every denomination; add to this a silver dollar, and a golden dollar. Fill a bowl, cauldron, or cup with rainwater and set it on your altar or magical workspace. Light two candles—use colors that represent the sun and the moon to you, and set them on either side of the container you are using.

Drop one coin into the water at a time, saying, "Night and day, sun and moon, abundance coming to me soon, never stop, these coins I drop, night and day, sun and moon."

Set your container of water with the coins to bask in the full moon's light. The next days, set the coins on your altar, or gather them in a cloth bag to a place near your workspace, wallet, or computer.

## One or the Other Candle Spell

If you have a question or two things you need to make a choice from, pick a candle in a color appropriate to your concern, and make sure it is not a "dripless" candle. Set it on a dish, and place a nickel on one side of the candle, a penny on the other. Designate which coin represents which choice; if this is a simple yes or no question then the penny is yes and the nickel is no. Anoint the candle in rosemary, lavender, or simply olive oil and light it, focusing your mind on the choices in front of you.

Speak your question, and ask the god and goddess to allow the candle to answer it for you.

Let the candle burn out until it's finished, and examine which coin has attracted the most wax: that is your answer.

## Protection Spell for the Home

This can also be considered a "spiritual cleansing" spells. Just like our carpets and our floors, our homes can get a lot of tracked in "spiritual dirt", over time. After guests visit or a repair person has come to fix the sink or just the simple act of you and your family coming home day after day, bringing with you the residual negativity of the outside world, it eventually will become necessary to sweep out the clutter so your unique, positive energy can shine through.

You'll want to gather four mason jars with lids that shut tight, some rice, lavender, and basil, as well as kosher salt for this spell.

**A note on spiritual cleansing.** Whether it's yourself, your house, a magical tool, or a piece of antique jewelry you found in a thrift store, mundane cleansing should always come before spiritual. Before you take a ritual bath, take a regular shower. Before you bless that vintage silver ring, polish it. Before you smudge your house, sweep it up, wipe the counters, and vacuum the rug. Doing this the day before sets your mind at ease so you can focus on your magical work.

Fill each jar with a handful of each ingredient. If you have a yard or outside space where neighbors won't pry, you can set each jar beside your house on each side, going from north to south. If you live in an apartment or flat or do not have private outside space, you can set a jar in a room that corresponds to each direction, at an exterior wall or on a windowsill.

As you set each jar down, say, North, south, east, and west, I ask you goddess, this house to bless." Let the jars remain a month and a day, then release the ingredients (toss in the garbage, in compost, or into the fire.)

## Spells to Open Yourself to Love

**Love spells** are possibly the most common spells desired, aside from money spells.

You can find countless love spells promising to win someone's heart, rekindle cooled affections, trick someone into falling in love with you, sweeping someone off their feet, etc. What is the intention here? You might say, "to gain love".

What is the only foundation for true love? It's trust.

Recall the Wiccan tenet that we say in a circle and in performing spell work: "In perfect love and perfect trust." Love that is tricked into being will never be perfect or true. Love that is not based on trust is doomed to fail or fail again.

If you feel that you are ready to open yourself to a new romance, there is absolutely no reason not to do a magic spell to help you along with that. Consider it a pact with yourself to begin to be the loving, nurturing person you can be—and to also be willing to accept love from others.

These are just a few items that are useful in a love spell: rose petals, oil, or incense; rose quartz, hematite, amethyst, patchouli, rosemary, hibiscus, river stones (ask permission from the river goddess and spirits before taking one, and leave a gift of fruit or flowers at the riverbank), and Adam and Eve root (orchid root).

For roses, generally yellow petals mean friendship and platonic love, pink means new romantic love, and red means passionate love.

**A simple love spell is to cut halves of one red rose and one white rose,** tie them to make a single flower with string, then toss this charm into the water of a river, lake or waterfall, asking for love to come to you.

**Use rose oil** to anoint a white, pink, or red candle, and write the qualities of love you desire in a relationship. Fold the paper towards you three times and let the candle burn down upon it.

**Write down the qualities you seek in a romantic partner**, fold the paper towards you three times and bind with red string, then pin inside a red cloth. Keep this charm on you to attract the attention of new, true love.

**Carry a sprig of goldenrod** in your pocket to attract a love that will be both rejuvenating and secret (at first). Goldenrod is actually not a cause of allergies as many thinks, as its pollen does not become airborne.

**Take a ritual bath** in rose petals, a drop of patchouli oil, and set rose quartz in the water with you. Close your eyes and imagine a moment together with your true love. Repeat the words, "God and goddess, they and I, at this moment, I will scry. In perfect love and perfect trust, allow destiny to join us." Allow the bathwater to drain but save a cup of it, along with the rose petals. Pat yourself dry gently, allowing the residual bathwater to remain on your skin. Toss the cup of water with petals in a crossroads, and true love will come your way in three months' time.

**Tell your secrets to the river goddess.** Place the river stone you found on your altar. Write down your hopes and dreams about love. Write down good qualities you find in yourself, and also challenges you've overcome and bad habits you've been able to put aside. Tell the goddess that you are ready for love to come into your life. Fold the paper three times towards you and place it beside the stone. Whenever you need a reminder that you are ready, gently hold the cool, smooth stone to your heart, and say, "Loving goddess, I am ready for the love that awaits me," as an affirmation.

# Honey Jars

**Rootwork** is a combination of many traditions and magical practices, coming over from Africa and the slave trade. Slaves in America needed to hide their magical work to avoid punishment, and began the tradition of using magic to survive in situations that were often dire. Today, rootwork exists as folk magic, and its nature is to be able to use what's on hand to produce extraordinary money, wealth, or abundance spell, write your very specific wishes on a piece of paper with a pencil, taking care not to lift the pencil off the paper until the statement is complete, fold it towards yourself twice, and place it in the jar with wealth-drawing herbs, shiny things of gold or silver, such as coins, gems, or biodegradable glitter. Seal the jar and burn gold, green, or silver candle on top for seven days, then three days during each full moon.

## Grimoire or Book of Shadows

Your book of shadows is a place for you to compile the spell work you do, your observations during magical work, and inspirations, prophetic dreams, or anything else that you experience on your path in Wicca. It should be kept sacred to you, and private. Avoid using it as a mundane journal, and do not include negative spell work in its pages.

**Black vs. White magic.** Some say that white magic is ineffective and that so-called "black" magic is anything that works.

Recall how the words black and dark are not negative; they're part of the natural world (as well as part of our human world). So, instead of using words of color to discuss magic, let's focus on *intent*. Your intention is what carries through your magic on the tides of your will. If you have harmful intentions, it's best to focus on self-healing and reflection. Life is full of challenges, and sometimes we might be tempted to use our magical knowledge for revenge or to sway someone else to our side.

Magic aimed at another person is simply not the Wiccan way. Recall the Rede: "and it harm none, do what ye will." Think about this tenet each time you begin to plan a new magical work, for whatever you put into the world returns to you, threefold.

# Chapter 9: Solitary vs. Coven

## The Solitary Witch

Of the many traits and sensibilities Wiccans, as well as pagans, have in common; a stubborn streak of individuality exists. This is perhaps what makes a witch, a witch—the will to do as they will, that it harm none, in their own, unique way. Because of this independence, many Wiccans choose to practice their faith alone. There is a beauty in connecting to nature and the gods on one's own terms, following a path that they alone can hear. In this role, the new witch is very much a student, and the entire universe, their teacher. Even Wiccans with decades-long experience, however, can find peace and meaning as a solitary practitioner.

## The Coven

That being said, joining together with one's community can be a heady experience indeed. Group ceremony can be extraordinarily moving and affirming. Rites of passage such as initiation, wiccaning, naming, hand-fasting, and croning are celebratory moments that a close-knit, trusted community will gather around and add to the personal joy of the celebrant and initiate.

**Finding a coven** can be tricky, however, and finding an earnest group of folks that you bond with, time-consuming. A coven can be quite large in these modern times, but it can also be a small group. In the latter case, the personalities have to match each other, and not clash. A good place to start if you're looking for a coven is a pagan community group—not officially a coven, but a group of like-minded folks who come together to celebrate the sabbats and esbats. Social media and the internet is a great place to start looking for local communities near you. When you find their websites, read what they're the focus is: some groups devote themselves to worshipping the goddess only while others follow both the goddess and the god. Some are for adults only, others are all ages. Once you start attending a few public circles and get to know some of the people there, you may get insight into where to find an established coven that are looking for new members.

# Conclusion

Thank for making it through to the end of *Wicca for Beginners*, let's hope it was informative and able to provide you with all of the tools you need to achieve your goals whatever they may be.

The next step is to look at the natural world around you. How do you see yourself in it? In what ways do you see the god and goddess in the world? The best way to begin your Wiccan path is to realize that you are a part of the world, and it is a part of you.

Finally, if you found this book useful in any way, a review on Amazon is always appreciated!

# Wicca Spells

*Wiccan Guide for Beginners.*
*The Witchcraft and Magic Meditation for Moon Ritual.*

Wiccapedia and New Religion Starter Kit.

# Table of Contents

WICCA SPELLS .................................................................. 172

TABLE OF CONTENTS ..................................................... 174

INTRODUCTION .............................................................. 178

CHAPTER 1: THE ORIGINS OF WICCA ............................... 180

CHAPTER 2: WICCAN BELIEFS AND PRACTICES ............ 186

CHAPTER 3: THE TOOLS OF THE CRAFT ......................... 198

CHAPTER 4: THE GOD AND THE GODDESS ..................... 213

CHAPTER 5: THE ELEMENTS AND THE WHEEL OF THE YEAR ................................................................................ 224

CHAPTER 6: SPELLS ......................................................... 257

CONCLUSION ................................................................... 324

© Copyright 2019 by Rachel Herbs - All rights reserved.

The following Book is reproduced below with the goal of providing information that is as accurate and reliable as possible. Regardless, purchasing this Book can be seen as consent to the fact that both the publisher and the author of this book are in no way experts on the topics discussed within and that any recommendations or suggestions that are made herein are for entertainment purposes only. Professionals should be consulted as needed prior to undertaking any of the action endorsed herein.

This declaration is deemed fair and valid by both the American Bar Association and the Committee of Publishers Association and is legally binding throughout the United States.

Furthermore, the transmission, duplication, or reproduction of any of the following work including specific information will be considered an illegal act irrespective of if it is done electronically or in print. This extends to creating a secondary or tertiary copy of the work or a recorded copy and is only allowed with the express written consent from the Publisher. All additional right reserved.

The information in the following pages is broadly considered a truthful and accurate account of facts and as such, any inattention, use, or misuse of the information in question by the reader will render any resulting actions solely under their purview. There are no scenarios in which the publisher or the original

author of this work can be in any fashion deemed liable for any hardship or damages that may befall them after undertaking information described herein.

Additionally, the information in the following pages is intended only for informational purposes and should thus be thought of as universal. As befitting its nature, it is presented without assurance regarding its prolonged validity or interim quality. Trademarks that are mentioned are done without written consent and can in no way be considered an endorsement from the trademark holder.

# Introduction

Congratulations on buying *Wicca Spells* and thank you for doing so.

Wicca is considered as one of the fastest growing religions in the United States and in the Western World. Unlike what was previously believed, Wicca promotes harmony and peace. By reading the following chapters of this book, you will know the origin and history of Wicca, Wiccan beliefs, rituals, and ethics, and the eight Wiccan sabbaths as well as the esbats—rituals devoted to the moon and the divine triple goddess. This book will also cover what it means to worship the god and goddess, and what they represent in their various aspects. A thorough introduction to the Wheel of the Year, the meaning of the days of the week, and a full spellbook for both the beginner and expert practitioner of magic is included. The spells in this book include chantings, rituals, and what you need to perform these spells can be commonly found in the household. The spells in this book are so simple that even the beginner can easily follow them.

Spells for wealth, abundance, luck in money and business, self-awareness, self-empowerment, love, romance, being open in receiving love in one's life, invisibility, protection of the home, protection of one's self or vehicle, and safe travels are just some of the spells included in *Wicca Spells*.

*Wicca Spells* will ready you as you take a journey of a lifetime. You already did the first step by purchasing this book. Now all you have to do is take the second step and learn the spells.

There are plenty of books on this subject on the market, thanks again for choosing this one! Every effort was made to ensure it is full of as much useful information as possible, please enjoy!

# Chapter 1: The Origins of Wicca

**A New, Old Religion**

Paganism is a broad term that includes earth-based faiths and Wicca, a form of paganism, is a tradition of witchcraft. Essentially, Wicca is known as Pagan Witchcraft and it has been called as the fastest-growing faith in the modern world, outside of Islam. Wicca believes in pantheism or that God is all around and that God is the same as the universe. It should also be clear that Wicca is not Satanism, or demon worship, as others would like to believe.

The history of Wicca is a complicated subject. There is little doubt that many of the rituals and practices of modern pagans and Wiccans today share their roots with ancient practices of European and Celtic tribes, the trouble is that most of that history was never preserved to page. Spoken-word traditions were more commonplace then, with the exception of some Norse scholars and Christian monks, who preserved much of Europe's history in their hand-written books.

It is ironic that so much history was saved for future generations by Christian monks as it was the spread of Christianity via the Roman Catholic Church itself that drove the matriarchal, pagan societies underground and into hiding. Still, there is not nearly enough information on pre-Christian Britain and Ireland to firmly state that "new" religions such as Wicca have firm, indisputable ties to the "old" ways. It is a matter of faith and of the early work of authors and scholars in the US and abroad.

**Charles Leland** wrote the book "Aradia – Gospel of the Witches" in 1899, which focused primarily on the goddess Diana.

**Gerald Gardner** wrote several books on witchcraft in the 1940s and 50s, being a member of a coven himself. He often used the phrase "Old Religion" to describe Wicca and witchcraft.

Gardner, also known as Scire, is recognized as the "Father of Wicca". He was formerly a civil servant until he discovered the occult. Wicca spread throughout the UK when Gardner initiated some priestesses who then initiated new members.

**Margaret Murray** authored several books describing the "burning times" of European history when men and women accused of witchcraft were burned alive at the stake. While her theories are not 100% provable, her thoughts and theories, along with Aleister Leland's and Gardner's, helped to provide the foundation on which the neo-pagan religion Wicca was built.

### Survival In An Agrarian Society

It makes sense that modern Wiccan, a faith that honors the natural world and humanity's place among it, is derived from the real-life hardships and survival of people living in the agrarian cultures of Europe. Without a good harvest, certain death waited in the cold grip of Winter. The changing of the seasons fully illustrated to these earlier pagans how the dark defeated the light, only to be defeated by the light as the Wheel of the Year turned towards Summer once more.

Throughout history, humankind has sought to control exterior forces that would impact daily life. This is where the craft of spellwork and magic also originated. In Wicca, the philosophy exists that humans should work with nature, not against it—so Wiccan spellcraft reflects this mindset.

## A Difficult History – The Burning Times

The "burning times", brought to worldwide discussion by the author Margaret Murray and studied by scholars today, are thought to have occurred from approximately the year 1000 to the 1700s. The "burning times" occurred during the Dark Ages when witches were accused of heresy and burned at the stake. Because of this, some pagans and Wiccans judge Christianity harshly, but in fact, the Roman Empire and the spread of Catholicism persecuted many peoples, Christians of other paths included. It was a difficult time to be anything but Catholic.

Today, there are bumper stickers that say "Never again the Burning Times!" Wiccans fight for their rights to practice their religion. There is a sense of rebellion, of absolute, stubborn individuality that is found to be common among practitioners and devotees of Wicca and from which we can all take a lesson from today—no matter how much your oppressors try to control you, your life is your own. Hence the Wiccan philosophy, called "The Wiccan Rede": *Do as you will, that it harm none.*

## Wiccans Differ in Their Views

Part of the appeal of pagan faiths, Wicca included, is having the personal freedom to follow one's own path. Some Wiccans are monotheistic, in that they believe in one, universal force—the deities they worship are simply smaller aspects of that great force. Other Wiccans are dualists and worship the god and the goddess, the masculine and feminine energies of the world, equally. Still, others consider themselves polytheists, worshipping a wide array of deities from different world cultures.

Still again, other Wiccans consider themselves agnostic, seeing the various deities, the god and the goddess, as symbols rather than actual, living beings.

## Led by Intuition Instead of Doctrine

Because of the very nature of modern society—the detachment from the natural world, the push to consume more, the complete and utter disconnect from what makes us living, breathing *beings*, many have found themselves seeking something that is old and ancient. We yearn for the wisdom of our ancestors, tired of being fed shallow, commercially-constructed advice that neither recognizes the jubilance of the spirit nor celebrates what makes humanity so special. We are shamed, bullied, cajoled, and herded along to conform, consume, and obey.

Like other pagan faiths, Wicca offers a more natural point of view. It allows us to be ourselves and not live in shame of our natural human expressions. It also gives us guidelines to live well and to live lovingly. Because of all this, many people are drawn to it, finding a semblance of that ancient wisdom within its parameters and in its practices.

Wicca asks that you listen to the truth within you and also question the truths that are told to you. When the entire, natural world is yours to find the truth in, the answers can become much more clear. This newly-born, mid-20th-century religion may be steeped in the old ways but has both the daring and trailblazing spirit of the modern age.

# Chapter 2: Wiccan Beliefs and Practices

**As Varied as Nature Itself**

One of the most appealing aspects of the Wiccan religion is the fact that the unique viewpoint and expression of the individual is respected. Some Wiccans might be drawn to worshipping the goddess primarily and devoting their daily faith to the divine feminine, while some are drawn more strongly to the god and his aspects. Others may focus their magic and meditation on the natural world, pouring their love into their garden, or in the care of their animal companions. Others may thrive on community and seek to become part of a coven or seek formal training so that one day, they might lead a Wiccan congregation. There is no wrong way to practice Wicca, so long as the Wiccan Rede is followed.

Wiccans believe that through the power of will, change can be brought about through the practice of magic and that in essence, magic is a science that has simply not been formally studied (yet).

## The Rule of Three and The Wiccan Rede

Also known as "The Threefold Law", the Rule of Three states that whatever you magical work you cast returns to you three times its original power. This acts as a thoughtful pause for Wiccans, who do not work with any magical spell that might directly negatively affect another person. Some take it even further to a Buddhist-like way of living, and try their best to not cause harm to the natural world around them if they can help it by practicing green living, veganism, and reducing their energy use and carbon footprint.

The Wiccan Rede states that "do as you will, that it harm none", and again, this is both a free and open invitation to live your most authentic self while also being mindful of the rights of those around you to do the same. It invites the practicing Wiccan to be aware of the consequences of their actions and celebrates peacefulness and harmony, rather than strife and discord. It is similar to the "Golden Rule".

## Are Wiccans Witches?

Yes. A "witch" is simply somebody who practices the art of magic. It is a gender-neutral term and a fairly commonplace one. A "warlock", on the other hand, is someone who uses the Dark Arts and has nothing to do with Wicca.

It does not imply the type of magic the person practices, and in the case of Wicca, certainly, nothing that could be classified as "black" magic is practiced. Magic has to do with a witch's will and their intention. A spell can be cast with fancy materials or with simply spoken or written words—the tools and ingredients used in casting a spell are not magical (though they do have energy, which helps focus the will). The magic lies within the imagination, focus, and personal power of the witch themselves.

Not every witch is Wiccan, however. Witches are members of other pagan religions such as Druidism, Heathenry, Odinism, and Asatru (Norse), Stregheria (Italian), and Feri. There are many others, focusing on magic and paganism from cultures across the world.

## Wiccan Beliefs About Humanity

Wiccans also believe in gender equality and equality among all nationalities and races. The revere nature fully and consider humanity to be a part of nature as well as its protector. Wiccans have an open-minded view of sex and sexuality. Nothing is considered wrong so long as consent is given and the expression of sex and sexuality are sacred to the god and goddess.

Wiccans do believe in the afterlife, and they believe it is a place of everlasting peace and healing, often referred to as "The Summerlands".

## The 13 Principles of the Wiccan Faith

1. Wiccans practice rites and rituals, known as Sabbaths and Esbats, to keep in tune with the natural rhythms of the world, such as the seasons, and the cycles of the Moon.

2. Wiccans recognize that possessing human intelligence makes us more responsible for our actions concerning the natural world and environment. Wiccans seek to live in harmony with those things.

3. Wiccans recognize that as witches, they possess a power that most ordinary people do not possess, however, they also recognize that anyone with the desire and patience to learn can also develop this power. They do not put themselves above other people.

4. Wiccans believe that the power of the universe exists in a duality—namely, the god and the goddess. The masculine and the feminine are equal and the energies of both exist in all things and peoples. One should never be placed above the other. Additionally, Wiccans believe that sexuality and its expressions are both natural, and sacred.

5. Wiccans recognize different planes of existence, such as the material world and the spirit world.

6. Wiccans do not have a hierarchy of power within their religion. They do, however, respect elders and teachers of the craft.

7. Wiccans believe that religion, daily practices and lifestyle choices, and use of magic are all woven together as a means to be devoted to their faith. These elements, combined with wisdom, are what make up the concept called witchcraft.

8. To be a witch, one must learn, study, and practice. One is not born a witch because of their ancestors alone. It is a choice, and a path to follow.

9. Wiccans believe that by developing their own self-awareness, as well as pursuing a greater understanding of their role in the universe, their lives will be more fulfilled.

10. Wiccans do not possess animosity towards Christianity or any other religion—save for the disrespect perpetrated by these religions as demanding their faith is the only "true" faith and by infringing the rights and religious freedoms of the practitioners of other faiths.

11. Wiccans agree to gregariously debate the origins of their craft and its aspects and tenets going into the future. They are devoted to a peaceful discussion where no one member of the faith is threatened by another.

12. Wiccans do not accept the concepts of the Christian "devil" or "Satan", nor do they believe in the power of absolute evil. Wiccans abhor the acquisition of power gained by the suffering of others. No gain should be another's loss.

13. Wiccans believe that within nature itself are keys to their well-being and happiness.

Wiccan Holidays and the Wheel of the Year

Wiccans celebrate sabbaths and esbats, either alone or together with a community, coven, or congregation. The sabbaths follow the natural changes in the world around us.

**On Samhain**, October 31st, Wiccans end the year in reflection and by the celebration of beloved ancestors.

**On Yule,** the 21st of December, also known as the winter solstice, Wiccans come together to celebrate warmth and light, even though it is the darkest night of the year.

**On Imbolc,** the 2nd of February, also known as Candlemas, Wiccans recognize the first signs of Spring and celebrate new beginnings and the fires of creativity and inspiration.

**On Ostara,** the 21st of March, also known as the spring equinox, Wiccans celebrate the return of the mother goddess to the Earth, as well as the signs of life returning after winter.

**On Beltane,** the 1st of May, Wiccans celebrate the reunion of the god and goddess and the beginning of times of plenty.

**On Litha,** the 21st of June, also known as the summer solstice and Midsummer, Wiccans celebrate the world in full bloom and the sovereignty of the Green Man, the god of the forest and field.

**On Lammas,** the 1st of August, also known as Lughnasadh, Wiccans celebrate the beginning of the harvest and the sacrifice of the Sun God as he gives his body back to the Earth.

**On Mabon,** the 21st of September, also known as the fall equinox, Wiccans celebrate harvest, family, and home.

## Wiccaning

Wiccaning is the ceremony of welcoming a child into the faith of Wicca. It does not mean, however, that the child is a practitioner of Wicca by default.

Wiccaning is a combination of a naming ceremony and public celebration for a newly-born child, though the parents may wait to perform a Wiccaning at any point in the child's life. The baby is introduced and blessings are said over the child so that the god and goddess may welcome them into the world and pledge to protect them as well. It is similar to a Christening but a Wiccaning makes no guarantee that the child will follow a particular faith or path. Wiccans and other pagans believe that such a decision is up to the child, when they are ready, and if they are ever ready at all.

There are hereditary Wiccan practices—hereditary in its non-biological meaning—but no one can be called "Wiccan since birth". There are family traditions handed down from generations called "Fam Trads" but naturally, consent is an important concept to Wiccans and pagans. They believe that a witch is someone who says they are a witch; someone who has made the decision to follow the Old Ways and see where that path takes them through life. They also believe that a child is simply not old enough to make such important life choices. Many children will identify with the faith of their parents, of course, and even desire to attend public rituals or rituals in the home when celebrating the Sabbaths. But children of Wiccan parents are never forced, never coerced, and never made to feel guilty about their interest or lack thereof of their parents' faiths.

## Handfasting

Handfasting is yet another ritual brought back to popularity from older times. It is not meant as a legally binding ceremony but it is usually done in part with a judge declaring a couple married. Some couples, however, enter into a handfasting simply as a proclamation and dedication of their love and remain legally unwed in the eyes of the court.

During a handfasting, a couple and their invited guests gather in a place of their choosing—it can outdoors, in someone's home, anywhere at all they like it to be. Usually, a priest or priestess of Wicca presides over the ceremony and ceremoniously binds the couples' clasped hands with a ritual cord. Poetry or song may take the place of vows but couples often do choose to write their own vows to each other. Rings may or may not be exchanged, and drink such as mead or wine passed around.

Beltane is one of the most popular sabbaths at which to perform a handfasting. Many couples opt to have it performed during a full moon esbat as well.

## Handparting

During a handfasting, a Wiccan couple will be asked to pledge that they remain together "for as long as our love may last". That is to say, most couples understand that love is a choice, as well as an action. It takes work and partnership to keep a marriage or union going. That being said, sometimes people's paths change and sometimes that leads to the decision to have a handparting.

Being that free will and consent is such a vital part of the pagan faith, Wiccans believe that there is nothing shameful about a divorce. In a handparting ceremony, the ceremonial cord is bound once again, then cut. Another ritual is to bring a ceramic chalice to the ceremony, and then the chalice is dropped, allowing it to shatter. Each partner keeps some of the pieces to remember what was once true, and of their new lives ahead of them.

## Croning, or Saging

Croning (for feminine elders) and Saging (for masculine elders) is a ceremony that celebrates old age, and the treasures that go with it, such as experience, wisdom, and a life lived well. Covens and Wiccan communities will often Crone or Sage their elders as a way to celebrate this part of their lives. Wiccans treasure their elders, realizing that to live a life devoted to the god and goddess is both an act of peace, as well as an act of rebellion, in modern times where Wicca and other pagan faiths are still minority religions.

Cronings and sagings often occur on Mabon, Samhain, and Yule, when the Crone aspect of the goddess is celebrated.

Another reason to crone or sage a person is if that person is battling a serious illness, such as cancer. Such ordeals often "age" a person, both in body and spirit, and should they survive, they will still possess knowledge and wisdom that someone their age might not otherwise possess. Children and teenagers have been croned and saged because of this. It is also believed that this might give them the strength to fight even harder, as the community recognizes the incredible courage they possess in enduring such a challenge.

## To Choose a Coven or Remain Solitary

When it comes to deciding whether or not to choose a community to join or to practice Wiccan alone, remember that no one should pressure you into either. If a group seems to be pressuring you to join them, they are probably not the group for you. With freedom sometimes comes abuse of power, and unfortunately, some Wiccans and pagans do use this power to bend the will of others, though doing so goes against the god and the goddess.

A coven is usually a smaller group of people, who have learned that they work well together. It is usually composed of no less than three but not more than 13 members. They might get together once a week, once a month, or only on the sabbaths. They usually decide together what they will focus on and take it from there. A coven might grow, either as members invite trusted friends in the faith, or become families. When a coven grows to a considerable size, it might still choose to call itself a coven but it is now considered more of a Wiccan community. Such communities can be wonderful sources of networking, knowledge, and comfort to new Wiccans seeking advice in their journey in the craft.

Some Wiccans never choose to join a community or coven, and that is perfectly acceptable. Many online communities exist where a solitary Wiccan might share their experience, gain new knowledge, and gain a sense of community without ever having to leave the privacy of their own home.

# Chapter 3: The Tools of the Craft

**An Introduction to Wiccan Magical Tools**

Wiccan tools are used both as symbolic items as well as a means to direct psychic energy. They are used in modern witchcraft because of proponents of the Wiccan movement throughout the 40s through to the 70s drawing on influences such as the Key of Solomon as well as rural folk magic from the British Isles and Europe.

They are not absolutely required for magical work or ritual and some Wiccans prefer to always work with one in particular while some Wiccans use none at all. One benefit of using traditional tools is that they can help us feel grounded in the past, connected to witches who've gone before us, using the old ways of crafting magic. In the end, it's completely up to the individual what they want to use and acquire for their sacred, magical altar space.

A note: magical tools can be pricey so when you're first starting out with magic, don't feel pressured to have all the "right" tools. Magic can be worked with simple ingredients, or even no ingredients at all, in a pinch.

When you do decide to begin your collection of magic tools, there are many online sources of pagan magical supplies for convenience. If you have access to a brick and mortar pagan shop, however, take the opportunity to visit it where you can feel the energy of each tool in your hands and better determine if it's the right one for you.

When you do purchase a tool (or receive one as a gift), it's essential that you cleanse it before using it. You can do this by:

- smudging, or using a smoking bundle of herbs such as sage, rosemary, or palo santo wood to cleanse the tool in sweeping, counterclockwise (widdershins to pagans) movements.
- bathing it in holy water (collected water such as rain or river water, and a pinch of kosher or pink salt).

- spraying it with Florida water.

You can also consecrate your tool by using a sweet incense in sunwise (clockwise) motions, and/or setting it out to bathe in the full moon's light.

As a rule, keep your tools out of public reach and dissuade others from handling them, so that they can be infused with your personal energy only.

## The Pentacle

A pentacle is not a symbol of the devil, contrary to the beliefs of some. It is a disc or circle, made of metal, clay, even glass, that is inscribed with the symbol of the five-pointed star or pentagram. Wiccans utilize the pentacle in its "right-side-up" form, which symbolizes several things. It stands for the five elements: air, water, fire, Earth, and *spirit* (which is us, as humans, and which is what makes magic possible). It also represents a human being standing in their power.

Upside-down, a pentacle is not an evil symbol; it simply symbolizes the natural world: think of a horned animal like a stag or a goat. The Christian church aligned horned and hoofed beasts with very un-Wiccan figures such as Satan and the devil long ago but those views are not supported by Wicca. The natural world, the plants, and animals that live within it are considered ours to protect and defend. We have a responsibility to it. The Horned God, also known as Father Herne or the Green

Man, is originally a British deity and revered among pagans and Wiccans alike.

The pentagram is used frequently in Wicca to decorate sacred items, such as the hilts of athames, books of shadows, ceremonial robes, cups, and literally anything the craftsperson can imagine. It is inscribed on military tombstones in the US for fallen Wiccan soldiers since 2007. It is also the most popular item of jewelry for many pagans and Wiccans. The pentagram and pentacle represent balance, the elements as well as a quiet pride in one's faith.

When seeking out a pentacle for purchase, you may find some of them inscribed with additional runes or symbols. Make sure you know what each of these symbols means so that it aligns with your own personal viewpoints and interests before you purchase it.

The pentacle is also the minor arcana Tarot suit representing the Earth, wealth, abundance, and creativity. It can be added to any abundance or money luck spell to give that spell a boost of Earthy energy.

If you choose to wear a pentacle out in public, keep in mind that many non-Wiccans are confused about the symbol and may make incorrect connections to it. Feel free to explain to them the truth of the matter, or if you prefer, keep the pentacle out of public sight until you are in the company of whom you trust and feel comfortable.

## The Athame

It is a traditional tool usually used in Pagan and Wiccan rituals. The athame is a dual-edged dagger, usually kept dull, that is used to ritually "cut" energy. For instance, in group ceremonies after the circle is cast, sometimes there is a need for someone to leave the circle (it can happen to you at home as well if you forget one of the ingredients of a spell in the kitchen). The method to release this person out of the circle without needing to open the circle completely, and recast it, is to symbolically "cut" a doorway for them, then close the doorway behind them. For this purpose, the athame is used.

It is also used in sabbath ceremonies to represent the god and the goddess uniting by gently dipping the athame into the cup, for symbolism. Traditionally, athames have black handles.

Which element the athame represents will vary depending upon which pagan tradition you ask. Some groups connect the athame, like all other blades, with the element of air, representing sharp intellect and the ability to cut through the confusion with the power of communication. Other groups associate the athame with the element of fire due to the fact that blades are forged in fire and thus symbolize transformation. Which element you choose to link your athame to is entirely up to you. The athame is linked with the minor arcana suit of swords in the Tarot.

### Practical or magical?

This is also up to you. Further in the chapter, we'll discuss the *bolene*, a sharp knife used to cut cords, harvest herbs, and any other thing that needs cutting during a magical ceremony or spell. Some Wiccans prefer to keep tools down to a minimum and simply purchase a sharper athame and use that for both practical and magical purposes.

Another point of view comes from "kitchen witches", or folks who find their sacred space is best represented in the kitchen where they concoct edible potions, brews, and foods for magical and spiritual purposes. This is a valid concept and such a Wiccan may choose to use their athame in this room as they consider it to be their most magical part of the home. Remember that one of the most beautiful aspects of a pagan faith is the freedom and individuality it grants its practitioners.

The athames available today, either from online shops or from a local store or craftsperson, vary widely in material. Some are quite fancy, encrusted with gems or even fashioned from solid crystal. Others are modest and plain. This is definitely one tool that you can choose to best match your own personality, so take your time in choosing yours if you decide to acquire one. Once you've purchased your athame, you can use it to cast your circle by pointing at each direction, and you can direct energy with it to magically charge an item in a spell.

## The Wand

There are few items more iconic to witches, pagans, and Wiccans than the magical wand. It has been described in folk and fairytales throughout human history. It is the magical extension of a witch's power and is used to direct that power for a specific result. The wand is associated with the element of fire, as well as the suit of wands in the minor arcana of the Tarot, although some see it as a symbol of air. Whichever element you personally associate with it is up to you.

A wand should typically be equal in length to your forearm (otherwise it becomes a stave!). Traditionally, wands are carved from wood, and great care is taken to choose wood from a tree because of its magical properties. Here are some popular trees to consider when choosing a wand:

- birch – feminine energy, healing emotional trauma, spells for renewal
- oak – sacred to the god, good for divination work, increases magical strength
- elder – intuition, linked to feminine energy, blessings, connection to the fairy realm
- ash – beloved to fairies; connected with justice and the dream realm
- alder – strengthens connections to the spirit realm, increases healing abilities; masculine energy, protection

- yew – connected to the cycles of death and rebirth, All Hallow's and Samhain, long life, psychic visions
- acacia – a protective wood, capable of enhancing psychic ability
- apple – good for money magic and abundance, love and romance

Other wands are crafted from metal and set with crystals while others can be carved from crystals themselves. A length of bamboo makes a wonderful homemade wand, in that because it is hollow: it can be filled with herbs or a written enchantment, and with some glue, capped with a crystal or gemstone.

Finding a wand while walking in the woods is often every witch's first experience. Make sure to choose a branch that has fallen and take time to carve your wand, imbuing it with your own, magical energy.

## The Cauldron

The cauldron is a pot-like or kettle-like bowl commonly used in spells, rituals, and scrying. It is also typically used with open fire. The cauldron can be considered even more iconic than the wand in history and folklore, though most of us will never be so lucky as to acquire a full-sized one. Now, tiny cauldrons are sold in pagan supply shops, just big enough to hold in one's hands, or set a candle in, or use for divination such as water-gazing.

Because of its associations to transformation and the womb, the cauldron is sacred to the goddess. It is typically aligned with the element of water, but some see it connected to fire as well. The cauldron is not necessarily considered essential to modern magical work but it can prove to be extremely useful; it is a fire-safe place to burn items such as candles, incense, herbs, and pieces of paper that you've written sigils or spells on. Fill it with water and it becomes a powerful symbol of abundance and creative potential. Gaze at the full moon on the water's surface, and it can be used for divination. Additionally, a cauldron is just an all-around satisfying item to have and to work with. They can be a little on the costly side, however, so take that into consideration before deciding to purchase one.

If you would like a cauldron as a symbolic tool for a spell or ritual but can't afford one, a bowl makes a perfectly good substitute.

### The Cup

This tool also called the chalice or the goblet, is linked with the minor arcana suit of cups in the Tarot. Like the cups suit, the magical tool that is the cup is associated with fertility, creativity, emotions, and abundance. It is very much like the major arcana card of the Empress—the cup represents what is joyful in life. It is also linked to the fertility and sensuality of the goddess, as well as the divine feminine.

The most traditional material for the cup is silver, linked with the Moon and the femininity of the goddess. The cup can be any material the craftsperson dreams of, however, and cups can be found made from wood, ceramic, stone, and minerals. A cup can be fanciful and formal or humble and plain.

An important thing to keep in mind when purchasing a cup is whether or not the material used is food-safe—one of the things a cup is used for most is for communal drink during a community celebration on a sabbath. Even if you just use it for personal ritual, it is best to ensure that it's safe to drink from.

An attractive-looking water or wine goblet purchased from a thrift store will make a suitable cup and have the added benefit of reuse and recycling a discarded item. Plastic is not recommended in magical ritual, however, as it is not friendly to the Earth.

Once a cup becomes a dedicated magical tool, keep it as such—don't use it for everyday meals.

### The Boline

The boline is the practical knife among magical Wiccan tools. It is used to cut plants, ritual food, carve letters into candles and wooden implements as well as cords when performing cord magic or ceremonies such as the Parting of Ways (a Wiccan's version of a divorce). Some Wiccans prefer to have both the boline and the athame, others prefer to have one. The choice is yours. If you plan on using your boline to occasionally cut food, make sure it is food-safe. Traditionally, bolines have white handles (unlike athames) but any knife can be used as a boline. Aside from kitchen witchery, it is still best to keep your boline apart from your mundane, household tools. While it serves a practical purpose, that purpose is still magical in nature.

## The Besom

The besom, or broom, is yet another iconic symbol of witchcraft. It was traditionally crafted from birch or ash but now can be crafted from any wood you desire, including corn stalks or palm leaves. The broom has been linked to witches throughout human history, and many believed that witches could fly upon their brooms—this legend was likely a misinterpretation of early pagans using astral projection or meditation to reach a higher state of consciousness.

The besom is not a tool that is used during ritual or ceremony at the altar. It is, however, used to magically "clean" a space and can be used during the ritual of spiritually cleansing a house or room. It "sweeps" out the negative energy so that the positive energy can fill a space.

Additionally, Wiccans who are "handfasting", or getting married within the Wiccan faith, often choose to perform the ritual of "jumping the broom".

The general rule of thumb with besoms is a practical, household broom can be used as a besom but a besom should never be used as a household broom. Allow your besom to be used for spiritual cleansing only so that its sacred energies will not be mingled with normal, everyday dirt.

### The Stave or Stang

The stave is a stick that a witch finds when wandering close to their home, from the woods or fields nearby. It is a forked stick and serves to connect the witch with the nature spirits of that area. Wiccans often collect a stave or stang each time they move to a new home, as a reminder of the home they left behind.

A practical use of a stave is to hold one's bag of items during a community ceremony or outdoor ritual: leaned against a tree or drive into the ground, it makes a handy place to hang a garment or parcel.

### The Bell

Bells are used throughout the world and among many different faiths. The magic of sound and tonal vibrations has been practiced and studied throughout human history. The ring of a bell has the instant effect of calming one's mind or alerting one to the beginning of ritual, magic, or prayer.

The bell can be used at many different points in ritual. It can be used before a spell is begun, in order to simultaneously cleanse and sanctify a sacred space. It can be used to call the spirits or deities closer to the circle. It can also be used to seal the spell, signaling its release into the universe, set on its own momentum.

There are some Wiccans who connect the bell with the element of air as it is through air that sound travels; however, others connect it with the element of water. Sound travels through water as well and sound waves look very much like the waves of the ocean when studied.

The bell is a wonderful tool to signal a single point of any ritual: casting a circle, drawing down the moon's energy into a circle, opening a circle, a call for a community to stand before a ritual. It is a lovely instrument that can add the beauty of sonic magic to a ceremony.

## The Book of Shadows

A Wiccan's book of shadows is a journal wherein they record their experiences during magical work, spells they've learned or written, and other things related to their journey as a witch. It should never contain ill-will, hexes or mundane matters such as shopping lists. It is a sacred book and can be kept on the altar.

## The Wiccan Altar

The altar is the sacred workspace, the focal center of magical work and the celebration of the sabbaths and esbats. In a community setting, it may be a table set in the woods, with dozens of candles burning and offerings from each member of the coven or community, adorned with decoration appropriate to the season and date. In a solitary witch's home, an altar will have representations of the god and goddess, and perhaps a space for ancestor worship as well as a place for magical tools such as the athame, bell, boline, cup, pentacle, wand, and cauldron. An altar does not have to conform to any set design—it is completely up to the community or individual how they choose to adorn it. The traditional setup, however, goes as thus:

On the lefthand side of the altar, images of the goddess as well as tools linked to her are placed—on the righthand side goes items and images of the god. Items representing the four elements (the witch themselves often is what will represent spirit) are placed as such: Earth at the head of the altar, Air on the righthand side, Fire at the base of the altar, Water on the lefthand side, assuming your altar is facing North.

**Personal taste.** There is no "correct" way to set up an altar and many Wiccans have a piece of furniture perform double-duty as their altar space, particularly if they do not live alone or do not want invited guests seeing their magical workspace. An altar can be as elaborate or plain as the practitioner chooses. Many Wiccans enjoy decorating their altar with items pertaining to the phase of the moon, the season, the closest sabbath while others decorate it with a current goal in mind. An altar does not have to be fancy but it should represent the values and interests of the witch, as well as inspire their spirituality and imagination.

# Chapter 4: The God and the Goddess

In Wicca, two major deities are worshipped, generally—the god and the goddess. They are considered two halves of one entire being, a representation of the duality of the universe, the masculine and the feminine. Throughout the world, there are many names for gods and goddesses, focusing on whichever aspects they have domain over.

Not every Wiccan or pagan worships both god and goddess and it is their right to do as they wish about it. Some worship the goddess exclusively, others, the god. Some devote their attention to one particular deity, depending on their background or upbringing, cultural experiences, or merely just a calling upon their intuition by that deity. Others worship many deities. It's up to you to take your time, listen to yourself, and decide who and how you will worship, if indeed you choose to worship at all. Such is the liberty that Wicca provides.

**The Triple Goddess**

The goddess herself is thought to be comprised of three main aspects, the maiden, mother, and crone. This is syncretized with the fact that the divine feminine mirrors humanity's ability to create life, and as such, life is often marked by certain milestones: childhood, coming-of-age, motherhood, reaching maturity, and the wisdom of age.

Regardless of the aspects of fertility, childbirth, and procreation, the triple goddess and her three forms have meaning and messages for everyone, young or old, regardless of gender.

A popular symbol for Wiccans and often used in jewelry is the symbol for the triple goddess: a full moon bracketed by a waning and waxing crescent.

### The Maiden

The Maiden is symbolized by the time of the new moon and waxing moon. She represents the power of youth, as well as beauty, hope, the power of faith and belief, and the ability to see the bright side of things. She is the brave hunter as aspected by Artemis, the beautiful nymph of Aphrodite, the lover of life and excitement as seen in Oshun. The Maiden doesn't merely represent sexual virginity—that is more of a human construct than anything else—instead, the Maiden represents the individual, free to walk the world in search of knowledge, adventure, and experience.

Some maiden goddesses are: (Artemis and Oshun), Parvati, Rhiannon, Diana, Brigid, Kore, Freya, Nimue, and Persephone. The colors of the maiden are white, pink, and pale blue.

The Maiden is curious, daring, and will often seek *you* out if there's something you're ignoring that needs your attention such as an opportunity or a decision that will bring positive results. Whenever you are in need of a helpmate in your endeavors, you can call upon the Maiden to work by your side. She is full of enthusiasm and unstoppable energy.

The Maiden answers only to herself. She is a protector of men, women, and children alike. The Maiden may also appear to you when you are in need of a shield maiden; when the forces of the world are simply overwhelming and you feel you have no one to turn to.

The Maiden is also good at getting us to recognize when we are forgetting to take a moment to stop and enjoy life's simple pleasures. She wants us to run barefoot on the grass, gaze at the flowing river, dance in the moonlight, wake up with the dawn.

The Maiden is also the protector of animals. While she represents the hunter, she does not abide by senseless killing. Instead, she is more of a woodsman and an expert of nature. Flowers sacred to her are any white flowers, and the owl and bear are also sacred to the Maiden.

The sabbaths of Imbolc and Ostara are sacred to the Maiden. At Yule, all three aspects of the goddess are celebrated.

### The Mother

The Mother aspect of the goddess is the most commonly-worshipped aspect. Here we see the goddess as giver and sustainer of life, providing us with abundance, nourishment, motherly healing, and empathy, as well as stern guidance when we need it. Some mother goddesses are sweet, patient and kind, others are also loving but firmer, directing us to the proper path to ensure our utmost happiness.

In this aspect, the goddess becomes the well-spring of life and the provider. She is at her highest physical power, represented by the height of summer and the laden fruit trees, and tall, waving crops of grains. The Mother brings balance and a sense of satisfaction to us—life is abundant, we are worthy of happiness, and all is well.

The color red is associated with the Mother goddess as it obviously conveys the blood of the menstrual cycle and of the womb. She gives us her lifeblood that we may carry on our own bloodlines. Blue is another color associated with the Mother goddess, as with Yemaya, a beloved goddess of the ocean worshipped in Nigeria, the Americas, and the Caribbean. Animals beloved to the Mother are pregnant animals, the dove, and deer.

While the Maiden is more of an inspirer, cohort, and adventure companion, the Mother goddess is here to guide us in life and often help us make difficult decisions. Just like a mother, she wants what is best for us, and seeks to show us the way in moments of miraculous, loving kindness. When we feel like we can't go any further, the Mother goddess will draw near, allows us to cry against her mantle of stars, and soothe our pains and hurts while inspiring us to draw more strength and soldier on.

She will work with you to avoid the pitfalls of addiction and excess. You will see clearly within her light what changes you need to make in your life to bring happiness, harmony, and peace to your days, as well as your nights.

The Mother goddess is most powerful during the full moon. Perform magic for abundance, self-love, healing, and personal strength when calling to the Mother goddess. Ask for her help with marriage, childbirth and fertility, life partners, caring for your animals and garden, making important life decisions, and help with awakening your natural spirituality.

The sabbaths of Beltane, Litha, and Lammas are sacred to the goddess in her Mother aspect.

Some Mother goddesses are: Bast, Ceres, Corn Mother, Frigg, Hathor, Isis, Macha, and Venus.

## The Crone

The Crone is often overlooked by practitioners of witchcraft and Wicca, but *she* is the one we should be listening to the most when it comes to magic. The Crone represents the wise woman, the shamanic healer, and the witch. She has lived a full life and has plenty of information to share, to help us get the "edge" on situations and gain the advantages that wisdom provides. She is a survivor and knows both love and pain. She is a healer of the most expert degree. She has knowledge of every herb, flower, tree, and animal on Earth, and can help you gain that knowledge as well. The Crone is a sorceress and brings us the gift of the magical arts.

The Crone is the aspect that has been the most caricatured throughout the history of pagan faiths. She has been called Evil Witch, Old Hag, and the Dark Goddess. The Crone stands at the crossroads between the living and the dead. She understands that death is nothing to be afraid of, and is only a beginning, and not an end. She lifts the veil for us and invites us to have a look, giving us courage as we hold her thin, wizened hand. With the Crone by our side, we can look at life in a completely different way, slow down a little, and deeply understand things we may have once taken for granted.

The Crone's color is black, representing the fact that black absorbs the full spectrum of the rainbow. Her darkness is both creative as well as destructive—creative in that from nothing comes something, from the womb comes life, from the darkness of space is born new stars—and destructive in that in time, all things must end, so that they may be reborn, recycled, repurposed and born again.

The Crone rules over Mabon and Samhain.


Some Crone goddesses are Hecate, Baba Yaga, Kali, Lilith, the Morrigan, Mother Hulle, and Nepthys.

## The God

The Wiccan god is the counterpart to the goddess, representing virility and the masculine aspects of the universe. He, too, goes through stages of life, born as an infant at Yule, running free as a youth through Imbolc and Ostara until he meets his lifemate, the goddess, at Beltane. The god can perform many roles in our lives: he can be a teacher and master to our apprentice, he can be a loving, doting father, he can be a keeper of mysteries that guides us towards deeper enlightenment, he can be a drinking partner. The god's roles as father, brother, hunter, scribe, blacksmith, captain, guide, shepherd, master at arms, devotee of peace, and myriad. He exists in all of us and seeks to unlock our greatest potential.

## The Oak King

The Oak King—the counterpart to the Holly King—originated in ancient British tribes. Instead of thinking as the Oak and Holly Kings as two separate entities, they are in fact two aspects of the same god, the shadow and the light, the sun and the darkness, the summer and the winter. The Oak King represents abundance. He ensures the harvest and the hunt will be successful and is the extrovert who loves celebrations and communities coming together to partake of his endless food and drink. He is the farmer with dirt beneath his fingernails; he is the hunter taking what he needs to provide for his village.

The Oak King is a force of directed energy. He is like the arrow sent from the archer's bow.

The Oak King represents expansion and growth. His abundance comes from hard work, the force of will and of personality, of taking the initiative and going for one's goals. He is forthright and honest, open and direct. There is no guile about him. Like the sun, he shines brightly, showing his intentions for all the world to see. Brash and bold, the Oak King is not afraid of adversity.

Gods representing the Oak King include: Pan, Janus, Jupiter, and Frey.

**The Holly King**

The Holly King represents the darker, or waning half of the year; the Holly King is born in Midsummer, and grows to maturity to finally fade at Yule, when the Oak King is reborn. The Holly King reaches maturity around Samhain, and presides over the ceremonies of the dead. He is a somber, wise version of the God, unafraid of the dark and the mysteries that lie therein.

The Holly King represents many things, including the natural cycles of death and decay. He is the harvest and the dying of the Summer, the rich colors of Autumn and the crackling of a warm fire, the long, cold sleep of Winter, and the widening of the veil that separates the spirit world from the material world. His knowledge is ancient and secret; like the Moon, he leads those who are unafraid of midnight processions and twilight offerings.

If there was nothing but expansion, the world would be overrun. The version of the God that the Holly King represents brings balance to life. The dying plants provide nutrients for the Earth, and drop their seeds into the cooling soil so that when the Wheel of the Year brings Spring back into our lives, new crops, flowers, and seedlings will sprout up, enlivening us with hope and inner promise. The Holly King makes no apology for who He is: he is necessary and unrelenting.

The Oak King and the Holly King are both considered to be "sacrificial gods", representing the ebb and flow of nature over the course of the Wheel of the Year.

The Holly King's key words are: withdrawal, decay, release, rest

The Holly King's colors are: black, silver, crimson, and brown.

The Holly King's legends include: Santa Claus, King Arthur's opponent Mordred, the Green Knight, the Corn King, and Bran.

Food and drink to be offered to the Holly King include: spiced cider or wine, dark ale, meade, cranberry juice and dark grape juice, roasted meats and dishes made from gourds.

Gods representing the Holly King include: Anubis, Thoth, Father Winter, Loki, Ogun, and Saturn.

## Lugh

Lugh is a heroic aspect of the God who the Celts worshipped. His name is invoked in the alternate name for Lammas—Lughnasadh. His ceremonial death marks the beginning of the official harvest, and also the "dying of the light", as his name means "shining one" and he represents in this aspect the Sun, and the coming of Winter.

Lugh can be helpful when invoked to overcome obstacles, as he is a warrior god of incredible prowess and sense of honor. His symbols include the spear and the sword, or any weapon that affords its bearer a long reach. The raven, wolf, horse, and wren are sacred to him, and wrens will often sing upon a branch in a winter garden when someone in the home requires extra courage. Offerings to Lugh may include whiskey, wheat bread, blackberries, golden coins, and dark wine.

## The Green Man

The Green Man is the aspect of the god most concerned with flora and fauna of the Earth. He roams the woodlands and the fields, the rainforests, and the campa, the savannah and the tundra alike to watch over every plant and animal the goddess gives birth to. He is the archer and the guide, presiding over animal husbandry, woodcraft, and homesteading. He is the lumberjack and the stealthy ranger, the bold archer and the sly tracker. He is represented by both the wolf and the fox.

The Green Man is most active in summer when the world is full and life is teaming. He comes to us when we are in need of rejuvenation, or when we need to get in touch with the natural world. The god Cernunnos accurately represents the Green Man, as does Herne.

## The Sun God

The Sun god is one of the more important aspects in Wiccan mythology. He brings life to the Earth—without the sun, life would be impossible, and simply not exist. Even the tiniest, blind albino creature living in a subterranean cave that never sees light depends on the sun for its existence, because the plankton and microbes that drift through the underground waterways begin in the oceans, enlivened by the sun.

The Wheel of the Year celebrates the return of the Sun God each year from his journeys. Some sun gods are: Ra, Ogun, and Apollo.

# Chapter 5: The Elements and the Wheel of the Year

The elements are not what is to be found on the periodic table, at least not in this context. They are the foundation of magic within the framework of the natural world. Each element symbolizes a school of thought and a way to work with nature. Depending on what your goal is with a particular magic spell, you may want to choose a particular element on which to focus.

### Earth

The element of Earth is feminine and linked to the goddess, and represents ancestral knowledge, the imparting of wisdom, strength, our ties to the planet, and foundations. The Earth element exists in both the ground in which we plant, as well as the seed that we place there and the tree that eventually grows. In this way, Earth can also be tied to growth and transformation, but in a slow, patient way—unlike the faster transformation that is represented by Fire. Earth is also connected to abundance and prosperity. The Queen of Pentacles minor arcana tarot card, as well as the Empress major arcana tarot card, manifest these beautifully. Earth magic is magic performed with an eye to the future, reaping what we've sown, planting a forest for future generations, and diligently working the fields while others play because the harvest will come soon enough, and after that—winter.

Earth spirit guides and beings include the stag, the bull, the wolf, and the beetle. Gods of the earth included Cernunnos, the horned god of the forest and Chronos. Goddesses of the earth include Gaea, and Demeter, goddess of the harvest.

The season the element of Earth represents is Winter. Its zodiac signs are Capricorn, Taurus, and Virgo. The time of day represented by Earth is midnight.

Some of the crystals that represent the element of Earth are: salt, petrified wood, amber, obsidian, onyx, and tiger's eye. Some of the herbs representing the element of Earth are: sage, pennyroyal, cinquefoil, rue.

Invoke the guardians of Earth for grounding energy, linking to the ancestors, garden and plant magic, protection.

Earth Magic:

- Cast a prosperity spell using a potato that's sprouted: enchant the potato with what you wish to harvest and plant it. Enchant the soil to deliver your wish. As the vine grows, add more enchanted soil. When the pot is full, abundance (and potatoes!) will be yours.
- Take time to stand barefoot on the ground. Allow the negativity that you've absorbed throughout the day and

week to flow back into the Earth, where the goddess can purify and recycle it into positive energy. It is important to ground oneself regularly.

- Acorn magic: bless and acorn and carry it for luck with money.

- Visit a riverbank. Earth and Water have a deep connection. Watch the water flow to teach you patience: a river can carve roads through a mountain.

**Air**

The element of air represents intellect, the powers of the mind, and logical thought. It is involved in communication, divination, augury (the practice of reading signs delivered by the activities and songs of birds), writing, sigil-magic, and song composition. It is a direct, masculine energy, and its corner on the compass is the East. Spells that have to do with personal freedom, clear communication between two parties, contracts, finding that which was lost, and journeys are the domain of Air.

Airy spirit guides and beings include the eagle, raven, and dove, as well as angelic messengers, and the Sphinx. Gods of the air include Mercury and Toth. Goddesses of the air include Oya, Nuit, and Ariada.

The season the element of air represents is Spring. Its zodiac signs are Aquarius, Libra, and Gemini. The time of day represented by air is dawn.

Some of the crystals that represent the element of air: topaz, white quartz, amethyst, labradorite, and citrine. Some of the herbs of the airy realm are: lavender, primrose, dandelion, and thyme.

Invoke the guardians of Air for swiftness in spellwork, clear communication, to gain hope in a difficult situation, and to expedite change and improvement.

Air Magic:

- Lightly tie feathers to the branches of a tree and fill them with your troubles. Ask the wind to blow your trouble away, then leave the feathers to be pulled away as the wind deems it so.

- Craft pinwheels in bright colors to place on your property; bless them for luck and as they spin, your luck increases.

- Consecrate incense with the power of air and light in the home when you're waiting to hear good news.

- Spend time in nature and ask Father Herne to ease your heart, then be quiet and listen. The wind should begin to gently blow through the trees, giving you comfort.

### Fire

The element of fire represents love, passion, inspiration, and creativity. We are fascinated by Fire, yet of all the elements, Fire is the one element that's too dangerous for us to touch. It is a gift of the gods and allows modern civilization to move forward, but is steeped in ancient ritual as well. Fire makes it possible to control metal through the forge; fire kept our ancestors alive through the winter. Watching a candle flame dance and flicker is one of the most potent meditative practices available to us. Jumping a bonfire was thought of as a magical act of courage.

Fire represents gifts that help us achieve the incredible but that also needs control to prevent disaster. Think of a careless, campfire spark causing a wide-reaching, destructive wildfire. In this way, Fire also represents unbridled passions. Sometimes, a little control is a good thing to exercise. Fire energy is masculine and is connected to the direction of the South. Its season is Summer, and time of day is noon.

Fiery spirit guides and beings include the Phoenix, salamander, dragon and firefly. Gods of fire include Ogun and Ra. Goddesses of fire include Brigit, Pele, and Sekhmet.

Some of the crystals that represent the element of fire: sunstone, garnet, yellow diamond, yellow jade. Some of the herbs of the fiery realm are: nettle, cinnamon, pepper, basil, and garlic.

Invoke the guardians of Fire for inspiration in creative works, as well as to ignite the flames of love. Temper Fire with water, such as having empathy when dealing with emotional work. Use Fire to bring hope into an impossibly dark situation, or to boost morale, camaraderie, and community circles.

Fire Magic:

- Light a candle and inscribe a wish in its wax, then meditate while watching its flame, slightly out of focus.
- Write your desire on a bay leaf, then toss it into a fire to release the desire into the universe.
- Burn incense to either cleanse or sweeten the energy in a home.
- Dance sunwise around a bonfire, calling to the god and goddess for love and light.

Water

The element of Water represents emotion, memory, and life itself. It is also a carrier element: think of ships crossing the ocean, or fishers navigating rivers in search of the day's catch. The element of Water is connected with the Moon as this heavenly body controls the ebb and flow of Earth's tides. Water is also a deeply feminine element, linked to the menstrual cycle and the ability to give life. As with any emotionally-charged force, the element of Water can also bring devastation, in tsunamis, floods, breaking dams, and hurricanes. Water is well-paired with Earth, a slower, more stable element, where the two complement and balance each other.

That being said, the power of Water to soothe is one of its most incredible features. Merely sitting next to a body of water and watching its currents can calm our unruly emotions; bathing in water can free the mind and body of stress, anxiety, and worry. The element of Water as Mother Goddess reminds us that we are never alone: our heavenly Mother is here on Earth with us, waiting to comfort us with open arms. Water is a feminine element, and receptive in nature.

Watery spirit guides and beings include the dolphin, naiad, nymph, turtle, water snakes, and sea serpent. Gods of water include Poseidon, Olokun, Hapi, and Freyr. Goddesses of water include Yemaya, Oshun, Tefnut, and Sarasvati.

The season the element of Water represents is Autumn. Its zodiac signs are Pisces, Scorpio, and Cancer. The time of day represented by Water is sunset.

Some of the crystals that represent the element of Water: aquamarine, white quartz, lapis lazuli. Some of the herbs of the airy realm are: chamomile, echinacea, kelp, rose, valerian.

Invoke the guardians of Water for connecting to one's emotion and memory, for healing, for connection to the Mother Goddess, and for the restoration of the spirit.

Water Magic:

- Fill a glass with water and breathe healing energy into it in a sacred space. Drink to calm the mind and restore and comfort the body.
- Spend time near flowing water for help with stress, work burnout, creative blocks.
- Cleanse yourself of negativity in the shower by adding pink salt to your body wash, scrub from neck to feet.
- Fill a black bowl or cauldron with water, and use its mirror-like service to *scry*, or see images that you can interpret to inform you of the future.
- Gather rainwater in jars to use in spells.

## The Wheel of the Year

Wiccans and other pagans refer to the changing seasons as "The Wheel of the Year". Throughout the pagan year, there are eight holidays, called *sabbaths*, that are celebrated by both covens and communities, as well as solitary witches alike. In addition, there are lunar-based days called *esbats*, marking and celebrating the ever-changing phases of the moon.

Wiccan and other pagan faiths do not have a lot to draw from as far as any sacred texts are concerned. As we mentioned, they are a "new-old" religion, built brick by brick from the experiences, insights, and actions of their practitioners and devoted faithful. On a sabbath or esbat, a Wiccan might choose to practice ritual in solitude but yet they know that around the world, others are joining them in spirit. This is a powerful link to community and faith.

Four of the sabbaths are two solstices and two equinoxes and linked with the journey of the Sun (the journey of our Earth around the sun, more accurately, but the ancient peoples we descend from saw it the former way). The other sabbaths are Earth-based, marking the changing seasons and the harvest.

The pagan year begins and ends with Samhain, one of the most somber but beloved sabbaths.

## Samhain

**October 31st – November 1st.** Pronounced as "SOW-when" is a religious festival that marks the end of summer and the beginning of winter. Samhain is a sabbath that connects us with our ancestors and beloved dead. It one of two times each year when the "veil" between the worlds—the spirit world and the material world in which we live—is the thinnest, the Springtime and Beltane being the second time the veil is thinnest. Wiccans and pagans in the UK and Wales have several other names for Samhain. For non-Wiccans, Samhain is popularly known as Halloween, All Hallows, Hallows, or All Souls Day.

One might think that a night to celebrate the dead is morbid but Wiccans use this time to mark the ending of things, such as the harvest, also. Death is a part of life and with death comes rebirth. In the summer, the god, called in this role the Oak King, gives up his life and body to add crucial nourishment to the Earth so that we might have a bountiful harvest. At Samhain, we recognize the symbolism of his sacrifice, and celebrate with a full table, including a "Mute Supper"—a plate set with food and drink for the god and for any wandering spirits in search of comfort.

Wiccans will often set an altar at this time specifically to honor ancestors and departed loved ones. Pictures of the beloved dead, flowers and candles, incense, and sweet and savory foods and bread will be placed there to show the utmost love and respect.

The ancient practice of carving turnips to place a burning candle within has given us the practice of carving Jack-o-lanterns out of pumpkins. The turnip is a plant connected with death and the spirit world; the pumpkin is a plant of the goddess, and of fertility. In this way, rebirth follows death, and the Wheel of the Year continues to turn.

Popular rituals for Samhain include a roaring bonfire and tossing wishes written on scraps of paper for the coming year.

**Colors for Samhain:** black, orange, red, white

**Sacred herbs and plants:** Rue, rosemary, garlic, foxglove, pumpkin

**Foods:** Roasted meats, nuts, root vegetables and leafy greens, savory bread and biscuits, honeyed cakes, sweets

**Drink:** Meade, red wine, cider, grape juice, ale, smoked tea.

**Goddesses:** Baba Yaga, Oya, Aradia, Hecate, Hel

**Gods:** Ellegua, Olodumare, Thoth, Anubis, Loki, the Green Man

## Yule

**December 20th – December 23rd.** Yule is the first sabbath of the pagan year. It occurs during the Winter Solstice and is the longest night and the shortest day of the year. It is a time when humanity comes together for warmth, shelter, comfort, and to remember that while the Sun seems cold and distant, it will soon begin to return. Yule is very much a fire festival as fire commands the power to banish both the dark and the cold. Candles will be lit at this time throughout the home and upon the altar, a bonfire is also lit, and torches carried over the snowy fields to celebrate the birth of the Oak King, and mourn the passing of the Holly King. In addition, this is the birthday of the Sun god. We can easily connect the frail nature of the sun at this time of year with a newborn baby, gentle and in need of protection.

The etymology of the name "Yule" is believed to have descended from Germanic ancestral tribes and from the Norse language before them.

Yule is very much a festival of lights and indoor gatherings will place dozens of candles to fill interior spaces with as much light as possible. Decorations of evergreen branches adorn the altar as well as images of the sun and solar symbols.

Many traditions and practices attributed to the Christian holiday Christmas are originally pagan practices, such as the decoration of a chopped fir tree, burning a Yule log, and caroling from home to home.

Yule is an excellent time to reflect on goals for the coming year as well as divining with cards or runes.

**Colors for Yule:** green, red, white, silver, gold

**Sacred herbs and plants:** Oak, holly, pine, birch, mistletoe, frankincense, myrrh

**Foods:** Roasted meats, game, nuts, root vegetables and leafy greens, savory bread and biscuits, honeyed cakes.

**Drink:** Meade, red wine, cider, grape juice, ale, mulled wine.

**Goddesses:** Isis, Hel, Hera

**Gods:** Odin, Ra, Herne, Lugh, Dionysus

## Imbolc

**February 2nd.** This day is also sacred to Brigid (pronounced *bride*), the Celtic goddess of fire, and to Oya, the Yoruban goddess of lightning, rainbows, the marketplace, and the cemetery. Imbolc is also called Brigid's Day and Candlemas, and Groundhog Day is also celebrated on this date. It is a time of hope because the worst of Winter is behind us and a small evidence of Spring are returning to the Earth. In some parts of the world, crocuses begin to appear at Imbolc.

Imbolc is a bright, uplifting sabbath when quiet celebrations of light and candles mark the place on the Wheel of the Year.

Wiccans will often choose this time of year for ritual cleansing to sweep out all the energy that's built up and perhaps gone stagnant after being cooped-up indoors all winter. Ritually sweeping energy out from room to room, as well as smudging or cleansing the air and floors, is a popular pastime on Imbolc.

For many of our ancestors, this time of year was when the first of the Spring lambs were born and so it is also popular on Imbolc to celebrate with dairy dishes. The altar and home are decorated with bouquets of Spring flowers as well and fires are lit in the hearth, as well as white candles placed throughout the house to welcome the Sun back and celebrate the goddess.

Popular rituals for Imbolc include self-dedications, wiccaning or naming ceremonies, and spells to plant the seed for a plan, goal, or dream to germinate and sprout.

**Colors for Imbolc:** white, lavender, yellow, pale green

**Sacred herbs and plants:** white and yellow flowers, crocuses, iris, heather, blackberry

**Foods:** Dairy dishes, egg dishes, herbed bread, fruits, sweet pastries, quiche, greens

**Drink:** herbal tea, white wine, cider, beer, white grape juice

**Goddesses:** Brigid, Oya, Persephone, Kore, Artemis

**Gods:** The Green Man, Herne, Ochosi, Horus, Thor

## Ostara

**March 19th- 23rd.** Ostara is also the Spring Equinox, and celebrated as the official height of Spring and the time when the sun is finally lending its warmth to the Earth once more. At this time of perfect balance, the forces of light and dark are equal, and our hearts and spirits can gain from this surer, spiritual footing.

The Oak King is growing quickly towards maturity and his eventual union with the goddess at Beltane. More plants are showing their faces from beneath the soil and animals are waking up from their long hibernations.

Good decorations for your altar at Ostara are potted plants and cut flowers as well as decorated eggs representing the fertility of the goddess and the growing life around us. The name Ostara originates with the European goddess Eostre, which is also the root of the word "estrus".

This is a perfect time for seed-magic: plant a seed imbued with your desire, enchant the soil and water it, and wait for it to sprout and grow.

Ostara and Eostre were also adopted by Christianity, and would become Easter, with all of its original pagan symbolism such as the prolific rabbit, and painted and cherished egg.

**Colors for Ostara:** pink, yellow, green, lavender, pale blue

**Sacred herbs and plants:** hyacinth, day lily, chamomile, lavender

**Foods:** Egg and dairy dishes, fruit dishes, fruited cakes, seed cakes

**Drink:** honey-mead, white wine, cider, fruit tea, lavender liqueur

**Goddesses:** Eostre, Freya, Saraswati, Yemaya, Aphrodite

**Gods:** Odin, Apollo, Osiris, Cupid

Beltane

**May 1st.** Beltane, also known as May Day, could easily be considered one of the most passionately celebrated of the sabbaths. It marks the movement from Spring to Summer, and the time when the god and goddess symbolically unite, both now mature and ready to procreate.

Across the world, bonfires are lit, maypoles with ribbons waving in the wind are erected, and in Edinburgh, Scotland, painted, topless revelers carry lit torches through the streets to mark the heaviest time of the year, full of delight in the expression of human sexuality, creativity, and passion. The goddess shifts from maidenhood into her role as mother now and the god is moving towards his throne at midsummer where he will be most powerful.

The maypole represents masculine energy and virility and is a tradition carried over from ancient European tribes. Celebrants each hold the end of a ribbon and circle the pole in an elaborate dance that eventually decorates the pole with a myriad of woven colors.

The name Beltane originates with the Irish language and was originally a fire festival. Bonfires are lit throughout the night to banish misfortune and illness and prepare the earth for planting by blessing the community for a good harvest.

Often a wedding feast in honor of the newly-wed god and goddess will be served at community rituals and all are invited to celebrate the reunion of the Sun god with his bride.

Spending the night out of doors is a common tradition as well as braiding one's hair and wearing wreaths of colorful flowers.

**Colors for Beltane:** green, orange, yellow, pink, white, purple

**Sacred herbs and plants:** cowslip, daisy, ash, lily of the valley, rose, angelica

**Foods:** Roasted meats and foul, vegetable and fruit dishes, dairy and egg dishes, elaborate cakes and sweets, wedding cake

Drink: all wines including sparkling wine, meade, dark ale, cider, sparkling grape juice, fruit punch

**Goddesses:** fertility goddesses, Yemaya, Oshun, Freya, Ishtar, Isis, Aphrodite

**Gods:** Sun gods, Pan, Cernunnos, Chango, Ra, Lugh, Herne, Apollo, Balder

# Litha

**June 20th – June 22nd.** Also known as Midsummer or Midsummer's Eve, Litha occurs during the Summer Solstice.

Litha is a time to celebrate the Sun God as well as the God of the Forest in his most powerful point. He sits on his woody throne and surveys all the thriving life around him. The goddess stirs within every blossoming plant, crawling ant, galloping beast, and swimming fish—her abundance is everywhere we look. The crops of the fields tower over us, promising a bountiful harvest. Life is very good.

This time of year, many Wiccans harvest magical herbs to dry and use throughout the year because it is at this time that the plants are at their greatest potency. The Sun is honored by keeping a candle lit throughout the day and a community celebration occurs at noon when the Sun is at its strongest point. At night, since this is another solar sabbath, a bonfire is lit to honor the Sun once more.

The traditional practice of divining one's true love on Midsummer's night is still practiced as well as spells concerning romance and marriage. Any area of your life that needs its "fires" relit can be benefited by magical work on this night.

At this point on the Wheel of the Year, the Oak King also begins his battle with the Holly King, who will vanquish him at Lammas, when he devotes his dying body to the Earth as the last benefit to a good harvest.

Other traditions from ancient Europe include rolling fiery wheels across the countryside, leading herds of animals across the last embers of bonfires to bless them, erecting bonfires to both honor the Sun as well as bless community members to keep them from illness or misfortune, and rubbing the ash from the bonfire on foreheads as a sign of being blessed by the god.

Magic involving protection of the person and the home is also an excellent activity for Midsummer's night as is the crafting of wands made from sticks one finds in the field or forest.

**Colors for Litha:** white, orange, bright and dark green, violet

**Sacred herbs:** These are thrown into the sacred bonfire: mistletoe, vervain, St. John's Wort, sage, honeysuckle, oak, sunflower, lavender, and heartsease.

**Foods:** Fresh fruits and vegetables, game animals, herbed bread, honey cakes.

**Drink:** Red wine, berry-flavored teas and meade, cider, cranberry juice, sparkling water, golden ale.

**Goddesses:** fertility goddesses, Yemaya, Oshun, Freya, Ishtar, Isis, Aphrodite

**Gods:** Sun gods, Pan, Cernunnos, Chango, Ra, Lugh, Herne, Apollo, Balder

## Lammas

**August 1st.** Also known as Lughnasadh, Lammas is a time of thoughtful service, sacrifices of labor and love, and the beginning of harvest. It is a bittersweet time when the sun still burns high in the sky, but plants have begun to wither from the heat, and we know that soon, the days will become shorter, and colder.

The Sun God gives his body to the Earth and is then represented by the wheat that goes into baking what is called "The First Bread". The Oak King finally succumbs to the Holly King who now begins to herald the coming Winter and his rise to power. The etymology of the word "lammas" is Anglo-Saxon in origin and once meant "the mass of loaves".

The god Lugh is thought to lay himself to rest at this time, hence the name Lughnasadh. Another legend holds that Lugh held a celebration to honor his mother, the goddess Tailtiu, after she succumbed to the effects of endlessly harvesting the fields for her mortal children.

Lammas is an important holiday in the Wiccan calender and celebrates an intersection of Summer and of Autumn. Decorations for the altar and home should reflect this: bright colors representing the sun and harvest as well as cooler colors invoking the shortening days.

A harvest feast, with bread as the main attraction, is a popular way to celebrate Lammas.

**Colors for Lammas:** orange, yellow, white, gold, red, brown

**Sacred herbs:** sage, rosemary, thyme, basil, mugwort, onion

**Foods:** Loaves of bread, cheese, apple dishes, gourds, baked pies, pork, mutton, and turkey

**Drink:** Red wine, mulled cider, ale, meade, sparkling fruit juices, fruit teas

**Goddesses:** Tailtiu, Demeter, Danu, Vestia, Pomona

**Gods:** Lugh, Herne, the Green Man, Pan, Dionysus, Saturn, Chronos

## Mabon

**September 21st.** Another name for this sabbath is Harvest Home. By this time, the harvest is in full swing, so to speak, and all are preparing for the coming Winter. This is a time for gratitude and reflection when the days are still somewhat easy and warm but the introspection of Autumn and Winter are upon us. It is a time to look back at the year and what we've accomplished but most importantly, how we have grown, as children of the goddess.

The veil between the spirit and the material world has begun to grow thin and soon it no longer poses a barrier when we reach Samhain. Memory and ancestral connection are strong now, forcing us to look inward for answers to questions only the spirits can tell.

Traditionally, pagan peoples will have just finished their hardest work of the year, the harvest. Mabon represents a time of needed and well-deserved rest, to kick back, and enjoy the fruits of their labor with family, friends, and community. Elaborate, generous meals, libations, and heavily-laden tables mark this time of year as well.

The ancient practice of carving turnips to place a burning candle within has given us the practice of carving Jack-o-lanterns out of pumpkins. The turnip is a plant connected with death and the spirit world; the pumpkin is a plant of the goddess, and of fertility. In this way, rebirth follows death, and the Wheel of the Year continues to turn.

This is a good sabbath for protection magic and the making of talismans as well as creating charms filled with joy and inner light for when the days become shorter still.

**Colors for Mabon:** brown, gold, green, red, orange, and yellow

**Sacred herbs:** bay, myrrh, oregano, tarragon, mint, juniper

**Foods:** Vegetable dishes, apple dishes, pumpkin pies, gourd dishes, corn, wheat cakes and breads, rye, roast meats and fish, candied yams and apples, sweet pastries.

**Drink:** Meade, red wine, cider, hearty ale, sparkling apple juice, cranberry juice

**Goddesses:** Persephone, the Morrigan, Pomona, Hera

**Gods:** Bacchus, Dionysus, Thoth, Odin, Obatala

**Esbats**

In addition to the eight sabbaths of Yule, Imbolc, Ostara, Beltane, Litha, Lammas, Mabon, and Samhain, there are what Wiccans call *esbats* or the lunar celebrations that follow the ever-changing phases of the moon. The esbats can be considered a second Wheel of the Year and while not every pagan follows them, they present many opportunities for ritual and magic outside of the major sabbaths.

During an esbat, the focus is, of course, the moon, and the goddess—particularly the aspect of the Triple Goddess. Communities and covens will often focus on one of the three aspects of the triple goddess for a lunar ceremony depending on the time of the year, such as the Crone aspect of the goddess in Autumn and Winter, the maiden aspect in Spring, and the Mother in late Spring and Summer.

Do not feel that you need to bring a specific deity into your sacred space if you are a solitary practitioner and wish to do magical work during an esbat. You may simply honor the goddess in general, and that is completely acceptable.

Most covens and communities celebrate one monthly esbat during that month's full moon, but an esbat can be observed at any time.

## The New Moon

The new moon has a unique energy that is often felt by those who are sensitive to changes in the air. It is a time for beginnings, for embarking on new voyages, actual or symbolic. It pushes the individual forward whether they are willing or not. A new moon might cause sleeplessness or emotional reactions. It is letting us know that the full moon is on its way, and with that, shifting tides within our hearts and within our spirits.

The new moon is representative of the Maiden aspect of the goddess. This aspect reflects apprenticeship, students, learning and studies as well as the hunter aspect of the goddess-like we see in Artemis. The Maiden is not always aromantic, however, and the new moon can also signal new love and the first signs of romance. The new moon is not only for beginnings, but second attempts, ascending to the next level of something, and breakthrough achievements.

Magic suitable for the new moon includes commitments to new starts, blessings for a new job, home, course of study, or relationship. Money magic started on the new moon and culminating on the full moon is especially potent. A simple candle spell: anoint a green candle with money drawing oil, and light it each night at 7PM, 8PM, or 9PM. Spend seven minutes meditating and imagining money coming to you happily, joyfully—do not wonder how or why. On the full moon, allow the candle to burn completely and tell the universe you are ready to receive abundance.

### The Time of the Waxing Moon

The waxing moon is a time of increasing abundance, growth, and anticipation that leads up to the culmination of the full moon. In the moon's cycle of birth, growth, death, and rebirth, this moon cycle represents new life in everything. It is a good time to reflect on what is increasing in your life, or what you want to increase. It is an excellent time to focus on accumulating wealth, readying oneself to experience love and romance, search for a new home, or travel.

Also, take a look at the negative aspects in your life during a waxing moon. This is not a good time to attempt to reduce those aspects through witchcraft, but instead, you can use the waxing moon to strengthen and increase the aspects of you that can help you rise above and beat those negative influences. Focus on self-empowerment, health, positivity, courage, empathy, and patience during this time.

Magic material gain, attracting new love, physical beauty and vitality, drawing abundance and good luck, finding opportunities, meeting new friends, bringing families closer, job searches, acquiring new skills and knowledge, can all be successfully performed under a waxing moon. Spells for growth and attraction are particularly well-suited for this time.

## The Full Moon

The full moon is the most potent time to perform magic. Its power naturally increases any witchcraft that is performed. In addition, this is the time most covens and communities choose to celebrate their monthly esbat, honoring the goddess in whichever aspect is best mirrored by the season. Sometimes, naming ceremonies, also called *wiccanings*, and handfastings, Wiccan versions of marriage ceremonies, are performed during a full moon esbat. This way, their special day is performed on an auspicious day but will not conflict with community ceremonies or worship during more important sabbaths.

The full moon becomes a powerful light that shines upon us, which is bringing many things into focus and up to the surface. It is a powerful time for self-reflection and revelation. The full moon asks of us to be honest with ourselves, but also to be gentle and empathetic. The moon is the goddess incarnate, loving and nurturing, ancient and wise. The goddess wants us to be happy and fulfilled. Turning to her in times of questioning can reveal possibilities you didn't know existed.

Any magic and spell is suitable for the full moon, naturally increased in efficacy and strength. Because of the full moon's ability to reveal truths to ourselves, however, any magic that adversely affects another person should be avoided, because the Rules of Three and Return will be increased, too. A Wiccan chooses to create greater peace and harmony in the world and doesn't actively choose to add to the world's strife or pain. Attend to your magic during the full moon with a loving, humble heart and you will receive great returns.

## The Time of the Waning Moon

The waning moon is a time of reduction, of things moving away, and winding down. It can be a good time for reflection for hard work when obstacles no longer slow us down. It is a good time for magical work involving getting rid of bad luck or illness as well as reducing something that's run rampant or gone unchecked for too long such as one's appetite, party habits, unrequited desire for another person, procrastination, weight gain, fatigue, or being the object of gossip.

Instead of looking at the waning moon as a time of loss, use it to your advantage. We are not meant to be in a constant state of reception and acquisition—sometimes, we need to be able to let go, shed our skins, discard that which no longer serves us. Just as the lushness of Summer dies down in Autumn and is absorbed back into the Earth at Winter so we, too, need to reduce and recycle some things in our lives that have reached their peak. It is healthy to be able to take stock of one's life and recognize aspects whose time has come and gone.

Magic involving protection, breaking bad habits, weight loss, eating healthier, getting an advantage over addictions, removing negativity, rising above one's enemies, and even monetary gain can be performed during a waning moon. Sometimes we get stuck in a rut and cannot see the opportunities in front of us. If you're feeling courageous and desire great, successful change,and perform a spell for an exciting new career during a waning moon.

## The Dark Moon

The dark moon's energy can be unsettling for some. Like the full moon, the dark moon is a mirror of the self, though it shows us our shadow side rather than the side the world sees day to day. A concept of a shadow self in Wiccan and other pagan faiths is that we all have darker leanings, habits, responses, or traits that we may not be proud of, or even ashamed of. However, the god and goddess support us as being our authentic selves as humans. They teach us that being human is nothing to be ashamed of.

Sometimes our shadows, when properly understood, accepted, and controlled, can be some of our strongest features. Doing shadow work under a dark moon is a way to courageously explore one's self, and come to terms with it, thus emerging stronger, happier, and more complete.

Magic to be performed on a dark moon may involve protection, invisibility, drawing the truth out from obscurity, raising self-confidence, accepting one's shadow traits, forgiveness of one's self or of another, making a pact to strive for something, and banishing negative energy from one's person, life, or home.

**Blue Moons and Blood Moons**

A blue moon is a second full moon in a month and presents a wonderful opportunity to perform magic that focuses on good fortune and luck. The blue moon increases the full moon's potency even more so nearly any magic focusing on positivity and gain should be performed at this time.

A blood moon is the result of something called a *syzygy* where the Earth, Sun, and Moon are almost exactly in line with each other. As the Earth moves between the other two heavenly bodies, its shadow appears on the Moon. This shadow is called an *umbra*.

A blood moon is when a level 5 red eclipse occurs. The illusion of the red color is caused by the Earth's shadow and presents an interesting time to perform magical spells. As the blood moon is the result of the Sun, Moon, and Earth joining forces, so to speak, so we can focus on spells that address our outer selves, inner knowledge and intuition, and how we are grounded in knowledge and experience. Breakthrough spells for career, a new book deal, meeting the lover of your dreams, overcoming a physical impairment, or any epiphany regarding self-awareness can be cast during a blood moon. Who knows—you might just win the lottery!

# Chapter 6: Spells

**Preparing To Work With Magic**

There are many things to consider when you decide to cast a spell. The time of day, for instance, as well the current moon phase, day of the week, and what natural items are available during that season.

When you're first getting started working with magic, preparation is advised so you have a clear plan of strategy. As you become more experienced, you'll find that you're more comfortable with "winging it" since you'll have committed to memory some of the things you've worked with in the past.

The number one question to ask yourself before you cast a spell is what do you desire to make happen, to change?

### Never Ask "How"

Your own attitude is perhaps the most powerful ingredient in any magic spell. It's human nature to seek the "how" and the "why" of things but when it comes to witchcraft and Wiccan magic, the only answers to how and why must be *because the universe will hear me and make it so* and *because I will it to be*. That's it. You are one being in a universe of energy. Trust in the fabric of things to fetch you the result you called for and let the questions leave your mind as you trust in your own ability to perform magic.

### Timing Your Spell

If there is a great need to cast a spell and time is of the essence, then by all means, cast it when you must. If you have the luxury of time, however, this is a guideline as to when to plan to do the work:

#### Lunar Phases

- **Waxing Moon:** Abundance, looking for a new job, looking for a new home, success with healing from an injury or illness*, new love, strengthening a relationship or family bond, spells to help a garden or plant grow, blessings for babies or young animals. *A healing spell during a waxing moon will focus on increasing the immune system, strength, or vitality of the person rather than focusing on the illness or injury itself.

- **Full Moon:** The most auspicious time to perform abundance spells, self-empowerment, spells for passion, success, beauty, spells for good luck in finance and business, blessings to consecrate tools, magic items, magic sachets or amulets, jewelry, crystals, potions, and elixirs.

- **Waning Moon:** banishing spells, spells to reduce the impact or influence of something, spells to cleanse a space or person of negativity, spells for help with healing from an illness or injury*, spells to reduce anxiety, worry, or depression. Spells to make things smaller and less significant. *A healing spell during a waning moon will focus on reducing the impact of the injury or lessening the infection or sickness in the person.

- **New Moon:** Spells for change within one's self, a new start, getting rid of bad habits and replacing them with good habits, spells to discern the truth of a matter, spells for commitment to a long-term goal.

- **Dark Moon:** Spells for protection, stealth, and invisibility. Spells for justice. Spells to honor the ancestors.

Days of the Week

- **Monday:** Spells that honor the moon or the divine feminine, spells for new beginnings. The moon's energy is full of mystery and it is the opposite of the bold, forward sun. This day is best for introspection and self-discovery rather than any spell that requires action. This is a good day for water magic, and the water element is strong on this day.

- **Tuesday:** This is a good day for spellwork involving self-empowerment and rising above or besting one's enemies. It is ruled by the god of war, Mars, and so avoid using bright red or any peppery spice such as cinnamon to ensure your magic isn't too incendiary. This is a good day to charge talismans and items of protection.

- **Wednesday:** Wear an item of red on this day for good luck. Wednesday is sacred to Mercury, god of communication. A good day for magic involving contracts, good news, good luck, and partnerships. A good time to do spellwork for financial success and success in business as well as safe travel and messages or work well-received.

- **Thursday:** This day is ideal for luck and good fortune spells as well as spells for abundance, money magic, and spells for good healthy. This day is ruled by Jupiter, god of luck. Also a good day for work involving justice and to gain favor with authorities. A good time for blessings of the home or vehicles.

- **Friday:** Friday is ruled by Venus but it is also sacred to other goddesses such as the Yoruban goddess of unbridled passion, the marketplace, lightning, and the graveyard. It is a heady day filled with possibility. A good day for love and attraction magic, success in attracting clients and customers, attracting the attention of someone you desire, and spells for beauty and self-confidence.

- **Saturday:** Ruled by Saturn, this day is best for protection magic, getting in touch with the beloved dead, creating wards of protection for person, home, and property. It is a good day for divination.

- **Sunday:** This day is, of course, ruled by the Sun. It is a day well-suited for spells for good health and vitality, successful planting, luck in money, and magic involving career and business.

## Understanding Your Intent

One of the most essential parts of witchcraft is having a clearly defined goal and intent before you begin. Take some time to write down what you wish to accomplish with the spell. The more specific, the better. It can be a series of results, step by step. Study your intention and determine if it's truly the right time to cast this spell.

**A note about casting spells on other people:** This is a subject often hotly debated in pagan circles. In Wicca, there is an explicit rule that you should not cast a spell on someone without their permission. If that person is in need of healing, encouragement, or better luck, a well-intentioned spell cast on their behalf is a good thought, but without their consent, it is a violation of their energy and their rights.

Additionally, spells to make someone "fall in love" or become attracted to you or another person are also against Wiccan values. They're also just a very bad idea. Bending the will of another person is nearly impossible through magic. The will of a human being is one of the strongest forces on Earth. The most common scenario that occurs as the result of a powerful love spell is an obsession—an unhealthy attachment to the person who cast the spell. This is not true love and it will not end well: obsession leads to codependency, or at worst, revulsion. The best way to attract true love is to focus on being the happiest, healthiest, most self-respecting, radiant person you can be, as well as being open to attracting love.

**When you're in need to protect yourself** or someone else from a specific person, casting a spell to create a protective barrier is permissible. Guarding yourself from negativity or ill will is not against Wiccan ethics, nor is a spell of return: casting a spell that returns any negative energy to the person who sent it.

## Preparing Yourself and Your Space

Before you get ready to cast your spell, take some time to cleanse yourself and your workspace. If you need a shower, have one—*then* spiritually cleanse yourself. It is said you "have to get rid of the worldly dirt before you tackle the spiritual dirt". Spiritual cleansing can be achieved by using sage, palo santo wood, rosemary, Florida water, or holy water (which you can make at home using nature-collected water such as river or rain water, and adding salt. Saltwater is also good for this). If smudging (using a smoking herb bundle like sage or rosemary), move the bundle counterclockwise (called widdershins in Wiccan ceremony) over the areas of your body, head to foot.

After you've cleansed yourself, do the same for your sacred space.

## Having the Proper Presence of Mind

When you're ready to cast your circle, take a few moments to ease your mind into a relaxed state. You may sit before your altar or workspace, keeping your posture straight, and breathing deeply, through your stomach. Empty your mind of thoughts. Just drift for a while, relax yourself into the best state of mind for magical work.

## Casting a Circle

Before you begin your magical work, it's important to enclose the space you're working *in*. The reasoning behind this is that you're about to use your own energy to cast a spell. There will be a point of focus, of some sort, that your energy will be aimed upon. A circle makes it easier to keep your energy in a small, focused area. Additionally, a protective circle will keep out any unknown, unseen, energies that might interfere with your work.

You should have a good idea where the four directions are in relation to your workspace or altar. Ideally, your altar should face North but if that's not possible don't worry. Another solution is to have a portable altar that you place in the center of your room when it's time for spellcasting. A wooden footstool or small coffee table works well for this.

Two easy ways to determine the directions if you don't have a compass: look up your home on Google Maps or Google Earth or download a compass app for your phone.

When you're ready to cast your circle, stand, and holding your wand or athame, point to the North.

*By the North where she dwells in power, by the East where she sings her song, by the South where the fires of her passion ignite, by the West where her waters run deep.*

You can add a verse for the god as well, if you like:

*By the North where he guards his fortress, by the East where he sails for home, by the South where he lights his fiery torch, by the West where he quenches his thirst.*

Then say:

*The circle is cast.*

Whenever you are finished with a spell, the last step will always be to recite the Casting Words:

*By the power of three times three, I cast this spell so humbly, to harm no one, nor to bring harm to me, I cast this spell – SO MOTE IT BE.*

When your work is done, you can open the circle by reciting the same words that you used to cast it, then instead of saying "the circle is cast", say "the circle is open, but unbroken."

### Grounding

One of the most important steps in magical work is called grounding. Your circle will contain an enormous amount of energy, and this energy will linger even after you've opened the circle. It can cause sleeplessness, nervousness, and restlessness in the spellcaster. It's essential that you *ground* this energy so it doesn't disturb the rest of your day or night.

You can accomplish grounding in a few different ways: you can kneel on the floor of your workspace, palms down, and feel the energy flow through you, into the floor, down to the Earth. Picture the room draining of the magical energy the way a bathtub drains water.

A second approach is to go outside, barefoot, and stand on land or rock for several minutes. Picture the energy draining out of you, down into the Earth.

## Candle Magic

Using a candle for a spell's focus is one the most simple and effective spells you can cast. Choose a color to enhance the focus, depending on what type of spell you're looking for. Additionally, when making a charm bag or amulet, consult the color guide when choosing the color of your material.

**white:** for a clear, focused mind, to purify, to cleanse, a neutral candle for any magic except banishing and protection.

**blue:** healing, obtaining wisdom, a peaceful home, patience.

**purple:** use for divination magic, prophetic dreams, creating peace between two people or groups, connection to the god and goddess, connection to the spirit world.

**red:** passion, strength, courage, robust health.

**orange:** success, good fortune, wealth, attraction, vitality.

**yellow:** sensuality, friendship, happiness, money magic, communication.

**black:** protection, transformation, connection with ancestors, enlightenment, potential.

**brown:** a happy home, prosperity, creativity, fertility, stamina, good investment of wealth and energy, spells for animals.

**pink:** magic for children and babies, angelic healing, spirituality, affection.

**gold:** financial success, divination, past life memory.

**silver:** wisdom, luck in love, invisibility, protection from negativity, psychic power.

## Spells For Personal Empowerment

### Earth and Sky Spell

What you'll need:

- bay leaf
- basil
- lemon balm
- a small rock of obsidian
- a small rock of tiger's eye
- a small cloth pouch (or you can sew your own if the latter then include needle, thread, and scissors in the items before you cast the circle)
- white tealight or short taper candle

Do this spell at night. Cast your circle, then raise your arms up, fingertips towards the ceiling. Feel the energy of the night sky, all its planets, moons, and stars, channeling down into your circle, swirling around until your circle fills with energy like water fills a glass. When your circle is full, imagine the energy glowing bright white, then allow your arms to drop comfortably at your sides.

Light the candle. Place the bay leaf in the pouch and say, "Tonight I give myself the gift of strength, and of endurance."

Place the basil in the pouch and say, "Tonight I give myself the gift of wealth, and of the courage to conquer my fears."

Place the lemon balm in the pouch and say, "Tonight I give myself the gift of love, and of success."

Place the obsidian in the pouch and say, "Tonight I give myself the gift of protection from negativity."

Place the tiger's eye in the pouch and say, "Tonight I give myself the gift of clarity, and of integrity."

Tie the pouch, or sew it closed if it's handmade. Hold the pouch in your hands and slowly move it clockwise (called "sunwise" in Wicca), above the candle. (Don't burn your hands).

Say: "Tonight I cast this spell for me, to reach for the stars and cast my net to the sea, to walk the Earth in discovery, to live my life happily."

Focus on the bag of charms, and imagine yourself in scenarios where you are happy, successful, and powerful. When you are ready, recite the Casting Words.

Inner Power Candle Spell

What you'll need:

- a white, brown, or blue taper candle

- a mixture of clove, juniper, and rose oils to anoint the candle. Handle the clove oil with care—only one or two drops of each are needed.
- a small, thin, paintbrush.
- a small dish on which to burn the candle.
- pink or kosher salt.
- matches to light the candle—preferable over a lighter, as metal should not strike a holy flame, but in a pinch, use what's available.

Cast your circle and draw the energy down from the universe. With the paintbrush, anoint the candle in the oil mixture, using brushstrokes that move from the back of the candle towards the front, and you. Work from the base of the candle towards the wick. Imagine yourself in moments of great personal power.

Light the candle and say:

"As it burns, so I learn. As it dances, so I turn. As it flickers, so I grow. As it melts, so my troubles go."

Move your hands above the candle as if you were drawing the healing energy of the flame towards you. Do this as you repeat:

"Flame of power, imbue me with your strength."

Sit in quiet contemplation for as long as your comfortable, imagining yourself overcoming obstacles, and obtaining happiness, and a peaceful heart. When you're ready, open the circle and allow the candle to burn down. After the candle is burned you can dispose of the wax and salt either by tossing them in a crossroads, or by burying them.

## Spell to Nourish the Heart

What you'll need:

- pink quartz
- rose petals
- lemon balm
- lemon essential oil

Do this spell on a new, waxing, or full moon.

Cast your circle in the bathroom. Fill a bath and add five drops of the lemon essential oil to it. Add the rose petals and lemon balm. After you've gotten into the bath, add the pink quartz. As you sit in the bath, close your eyes and imagine a pink, healing light gleaming on the water. Imagine your body soaking up this healing energy. Feel your heart glowing with happiness and warmth that radiates throughout your entire body.

When you are ready, repeat these words:

"I am worthy of love, and I am capable of love.

I am worthy of peace, and I am capable of peace.

I am worthy of happiness, and I am capable of happiness.

All good things are possible. May they come into my life as blessings."

When you're finished with the bath, allow the water to drain and pat yourself dry (do not rub or wipe) with a towel from your feet up to your head. Discard the herbs and return to the quartz to your altar.

Spell For Personal Success and Achievement

What you'll need:

- a piece of sunstone
- an orange candle
- pink or kosher salt
- juniper berries
- some soil
- a small bowl, or cauldron
- benzoin incense
- myrrh oil
- small, slim paintbrush
- matches

Cast your circle, and anoint the candle with the myrrh oil. Light the incense. In the bowl or cauldron, place the salt, soil, sunstone, and juniper berries. Mix these with your athame or wand, in a sunwise direction.

As you stir the ingredients, say:

"As the Sun warms the Earth and encourages the harvest,

so does my ability for success grow every day.

I will achieve my goals and dreams, step by step,

as sure as the sunflower and the wheat grows tall."

Picture the sun shining down on a field of wheat and sunflowers: these represent your success and finances. Picture the wind swaying the tall stalks. See how the field spans out endlessly towards the horizon. This is your success, it is tangible and real.

Say:

"As the candle burns its flame, so does my success increase."

When you are ready, open the circle and allow the candle to continue burning down. Sprinkle the spell ingredients except for the sunstone in an open field at your earliest convenience.

**Tiger's Eye Self-Esteem Spell**

What you'll need:

- a piece of tiger's eye
- a yellow, white, or orange candle
- matches

- a small plate or candleholder
- Solar oil: three drops of rosemary, cedar, and orange oil mixed
- a small, thin paintbrush

Anoint the candle with the solar oil, then light the candle. Stand before it holding the tiger's eye in your hands. Look to the ceiling and imagine the sun. Close your eyes.

Imagine the sun's rays filling the space of your sacred circle. Picture their warmth filling you, soothing every limb, filling you with passion, and with courage. Know that whenever you face a difficult situation, the sun's energy will be there to keep you strong.

Say these words:

"I call upon the energy of the Sun

to imbue this crystal

with your power.

May it be a constant reminder

of my self-worth,

each day I spend

on Earth."

Lift your hand with the crystal and allow the sun to fill the tiger's eye with its bold, confident energy. When you're ready, open the circle and allow the candle to burn down. Keep the tiger's eye in your pocket throughout your days or place it on your altar for daily meditation.

**A Spell to Reclaim Power**

What you'll need:

- white quarts
- a piece of onyx
- one white and one black candle
- matches
- Sacred oil blend: rosemary, myrrh, frankincense
- a small, thin paintbrush
- Florida water, or holy water
- bundle of sweet grass or hand-picked wildflowers
- a vase or glass half-filled with water

Do this spell on a waning or dark moon. After the circle is cast, anoint both candles and set them on your altar or workspace. Place the onyx and the quartz between them so that from left to right they look like this: black candle, onyx, white quartz, white candle. Take the bundle of wildflowers and lightly sprinkle them with Florida or holy water then shake the water onto yourself using the bundle of wildflowers, from head to toe. Once you've done this, place the wildflowers in the vase on your altar.

Now take the stones and hold them, one in each hand: hold the onyx in your right hand and the white quartz in your left.

Say:

"I take back that which belongs to me,

by the darkness of night and the bright light of day.

I call upon the dark moon's energy,

to guide my thoughts and light the way.

What was stolen is now restored,

and the balance of my mind returned.

By the magic within these stones,

and by the flame of the candle that burns."

Lift your arms, still holding the stones, and feel the energies of your life in perfect balance. Feel your power course through you like the infinity symbol, a figure eight—endless. No one can alter or stop this.

When you are ready, return the stones to their places on the altar, and open the circle.

**Simple Spell to Overcome an Obstacle**

What you'll need:

- small gathered sticks (you will need at least ten) from the woods: each stick should be approximately 5" long
- dragon's blood incense
- a red candle
- clove oil
- a small, thin paintbrush
- matches
- a candleholder or plate

Cast the circle, anoint the candle, and light the incense. Take the sticks and one by one, build a small structure. The design is up to you: it can be a little house, a pyramid, or you can stack the sticks five across going one way, five across the other. Make sure the structure is as tall as you can get it.

While you work on this, describe the obstacle or problem you're wanting to overcome. With each placement of a new stick, describe one facet or fact of the obstacle.

When you're finished with this work, say:

"By the fiery flame of this candle,

so I ignite my courage."

With one, strong sweep of your hand, knock the structure you've built off of your altar. As you're doing so, imagine your victory in overcoming the obstacle you described.

Say:

"And so it is done."

After you've opened the circle and allowed the candle to burn down, discard the sticks in the woods, a field, or at a crossroads.

## Spells For Wealth and Abundance

### Changing Your Mind About Money

Before you embark on casting a money spell, take some time to examine your attitude towards money. Unfortunately, many of us have a negative attitude towards money—even if we love getting money and enjoy shopping with it! Those of us who have a *scarcity* mentality are always worried about money running out, and who wouldn't be? Remember that magic is the exercise of will to create change. You can change your financial situation through magic, but you have to stop worrying about money being scarce.

Start changing your outlook today. Every time you spend money, be thankful for it. Actively thank your money for working hard for you—tell it to bring back its friends to you a hundredfold. Even if you're just paying your phone bill, thank the universe for allowing you to pay it, and thank your money for being there when you needed it.

**Bad ways of thinking to get rid of right now:**

- I don't deserve to have a lot of money.
- I never make enough money.
- I don't possess the proper education, skills, or talents to make the money I want.

Remember, never ask "how". The universe knows how—you only have to trust in your strong connection to the universe. If you contradict your magical work, it will fail, plain and simple. You have to change your beliefs first so that your will can create miracles through magic.

**Practice affirmations.** Anywhere from a full lunar cycle, to a week before you want to cast your money magic spell, take a few minutes each day to repeat a money-related affirmation, such as:

"I deserve to have the money I desire."

"I am good at making money."

"I attract abundance every day."

"Money is coming to me every day."

Try to stay in the present when you recite affirmations; don't make statements that pertain to the future. Stay in the *now*.

And even if you don't yet believe these affirmations, saying them every day will change your thinking, in time. You can choose to light a candle and cast a circle when you recite one or several of these affirmations.

**Practice gratitude.** When your thinking is gratitude-based, you will stop dwelling on what you lack and start focusing on what you *have*. Take time every day to say out loud or write down something you're thankful for having. BELIEVE what you're saying.

**Counter negativity with a question.** If you catch yourself slipping back into the old habit of thinking negatively about money, try this exercise. If you find yourself thinking, "I never have enough money," turn it into a question: "Why do I feel as if I never have enough money?" Take time to meditate on the question, let it remain in your thinking as you go about your days. Eventually, you will answer the question subconsciously and the doubt itself will disappear and will no longer rooted in reality. That old, negative belief will no longer haunt you.

**Orange Money Spell**

What you'll need:

- an orange
- a golden or silver dollar
- a small piece of paper and a pencil

- powdered cinnamon
- basil
- patchouli (herb), or patchouli oil
- orange zest, powdered or crumbled
- vervain
- a brown or green candle
- Abundance oil: a mixture of honey, patchouli oil, lemon oil, and sandalwood
- matches
- a dish on which to burn the candle
- a small, sharp knife

Perform this spell on a new, waxing, or full moon. Anoint the candle with the abundance oil and light it.

Write on the piece of paper: *money come, money grow, money dance, money flow*. Place the coin onto the middle of the paper and sprinkle the cinnamon, basil, patchouli, orange zest, and vervain onto it.

Fold the paper towards you, then turn it sunwise and fold it once more. Do this as many times as you need to make it small enough to fit inside the orange. Make a small, deep cut in the orange and place the folded spell inside. Place the orange on your altar and keep it there for seven days. After the seventh day, remove the coin and donate it to a charity. Discard the orange and paper.

## A Simple Spell For Abundance

What you'll need:

- your cauldron or a silver bowl
- three silver dollars
- collected rain or river water

Perform this spell only on a full moon. Fill the cauldron or bowl halfway with the collected water. As you drop each coin into the water, say:

"Abundance, come to me,

by river, road, air or sea.

I am grateful for this abundance, eternally."

Place the cauldron or bowl where the moon's light can reflect upon the water's surface. The next day, remove the coins and keep them in your pocket, billfold, or purse. Never spend them.

## A Treasure Chest

What you'll need:

- a wooden box with a latch

- a coin of every denomination, some foreign coins, and a paper bill of each denomination
- green jade
- pyrite
- clear quartz
- rose quartz
- a bundle of alfalfa, tied with green string
- freshly picked basil leaves
- three bay leaves
- a piece of ginger root
- Abundance oil
- Florida water or orange blossom water
- a spray bottle
- a bundle of sage
- matches

Perform this spell under a full moon. A blue moon (the second full moon in a month) is a particularly good time for this spell.

This is an expensive spell, obviously, but a powerful one. Save it for a time when things are going well, or—save *up* for it to build up your abundance and help keep it going strong. In the spray bottle, mix some Florida or orange blossom water with a few drops of the abundance oil.

Light the sage bundle and gently smudge each coin, bill, and stone. Take the spray bottle and lightly mist each coin, bill, and stone, setting each one inside the box as you do so. As you place each object into the box, say:

"By the power of three times three, this treasure box brings abundance to me."

When you're finished placing all the objects in the box, close the box and place your hand upon it. Say:

"This box is now a magnet for wealth and prosperity

which then flows from this box to me,

that it harm none,

so mote it be."

Set the box in the light of the moon, either outside (where it won't be detected or stolen), or on a windowsill, and say:

"Bella luna,

cast your light

upon this treasure box tonight

and let my magic take flight."

Recharge the box every full moon for continued flow of wealth and abundance. *Note:* if you ever find you're in a situation where you must spend the money in the box, do not worry over it. Use the stones in new ways for continued prosperity, and when you're able, refill and recharge the box.

**Red Cloth Money Bag**

What you'll need:

- a red cloth bag or pouch (small); you can also sew your own
- needle, red thread, scissors if you're using a bag you've sewn yourself
- three golden dollars
- a small mirror—small enough to fit easily into the pouch
- a green candle
- Abundance oil
- a small, thin paintbrush
- matches
- a candleholder or small dish

Do this spell only on a full moon. Anoint the candle and light it. Take time to draw down the power of the moon; holding your hands high, say:

"Bella luna,

come on down,

so lovely, with your silvery crown,

grace this circle with your light

bless my magical work this night."

Feel the powerful, lunar energy coursing down into your circle, filling the space with white light. Drop your hands when you feel the circle is full.

Place the three coins and the mirror into the pouch, then either sew or tie it shut. Hold the bag in your hand while focusing your gaze at the candle's light.

Say:

"Paper and coin,

abundance and wealth,

for joy, for freedom, and in good health,

is mine tonight, and forever on,

beneath the moon's light and the sun's,

to bring me no harm, nor to harm anyone."

Raise the bag up to the moon's light and say: "So mote it be, and so it is done."

After you open the circle, allow the candle to burn down. Carry the bag with you or let it remain on your altar. Additionally, you can place it on top of your wallet when you're at home.

**A Simple Candle Money Spell**

What you'll need:

- a green candle
- matches
- a dish on which to burn the candle

Do this spell on the full or waxing moon. Light the candle and very carefully, place your the back of your hand above it, just high enough so that you can feel it warming your hand. Turn your hand in sunwise circles, and say:

"God and goddess, bring to me $500."

Seven Day Money Money Spell

What you'll need:

- a green candle
- a white candle
- two candleholders or dishes
- Abundance oil or Wealth oil: cedar, frankincense, and rose
- matches
- a small, thin paintbrush

Do this spell on a waxing or full moon. Anoint both candles and place them approximately seven inches apart from each other and light them. Bring down the power of the moon, raising your arms to the ceiling and saying:

"Mother goddess, grant me your powerful, lunar energy. Fill this circle with your light."

Imagine the lunar light filling your circle like rushing water. Drop your arms when the space is full.

Each time you say the following chant, move the white candle, representing yourself, one step closer to the green candle. Say this chant seven times:

"Riches and wealth, come to me,

by the power of three times three,

to bring harm to no one nor to bring harm to me,

Abundance is mine, so mote it be."

Allow the candles to burn for seven minutes, then snuff them out by pinching the flame. Burn them for seven minutes a day, for seven days. On the seventh day allow the candles to continue burning down until they're finished.

## Spells For Love, Happiness, and Relationships

### The Heart of the Ocean Love Spell

What you'll need:

- A blue, green, or white bowl
- Seven seashells
- Seven pearls (you can buy a strand of pearls at a craft store—they can be freshwater or saltwater, either is fine for this purpose)
- Ocean sand (easy to find in the floral department of many large stores)
- A blue, green, or white candle
- Matches
- A dish or candleholder
- Pure Love oil: rose, sandalwood, jasmine
- A small, thin paintbrush
- Saltwater (you can make your own with collected rainwater and pink salt, use a teaspoon of salt in this case)
- A piece of green jade, or a moonstone

This is a spell if you believe that you are ready for a healthy, loving, long-term romantic relationship. You are ready to be open to receiving love as well as giving love, unconditionally. Perform this spell on a new, waxing, or full moon. Take time for this spell, do not rush through it. Have a soothing shower or relaxing bath before you begin.

Anoint the candle with the oil and light it. Pour the rainwater into the bowl, and slowly pour in the salt, stirring sunwise as you focus on your open, loving heart. Raise your arms toward the sky and feel the loving, peaceful energy of the moon pour down and fill your sacred circle. Once the energy glows the brightest, let your arms drop. It is time to begin.

Drop the gemstone into the bowl.

Pour the sand into the bowl so that it covers the bottom of the bowl but does not rise above the water. Say:

"Life is change, like the shifting tides.

I am ready for love."

Pick up one of the seashells, imagine yourself filling it with loving patience. Drop it into the water and say:

"Life is a test, and requires patience.

I am ready for love."

Pick up a second seashell. Imagine filling it with laughter and delight. Drop it into the water and say:

"Life is fun, and filled with friendship.

I am ready for love."

Pick up a third seashell, and imagine filling it with peaceful solitude. Drop it into the water and say:

"Life is sometimes a journey alone until we reunite again.

I am ready for love."

Pick up a fourth shell and imagine filling it with passion. Picture embracing your true love, and if you're comfortable, picture kissing them. Drop the shell into the water and say:

"Life will make me hunger for the one I adore the most.

I am ready for love."

Pick up a fifth shell, and imagine filling it with gentle calm. Picture holding hands with your true love, in silence, watching a sunset. Drop the shell into the water and say:

"Life is reflection, together with my equal in life.

I am ready for love."

Pick up a sixth shell, and imagine filling it with strength. Imagine hearing words you do not like, and meeting those darker emotions with a renewed sense of love. Drop the shell into the water and say:

"Life is an occasional struggle, yet I rise to this with even greater love.

I am ready for love."

Pick up the last shell and hold it in your hands clasped. Imagine a lifetime in moving images, happy scenes, scenes of togetherness, scenes of disagreements with loving resolutions, scenes of travel, scenes of accomplishment. Say:

"Life is a winding road that I will walk together with my true love.

I am ready for love."

Drop the last shell into the water. With your hand, or with your wand, trace a sunwise circle above the bowl. Say:

"These ingredients I invest in thee, like all the treasures in the sea, to one day bless us, you and me, together in love, successfully."

Reach into the bowl and remove the stone you dropped in the beginning of the spell. Keep it on your altar or carry it with you as a beacon to your true love that they easily find you in the world. Remember true love takes time. Allow the spell to send its message into the universe, and when the time is right, your true love will appear.

**Attracting Love Sachet**

What you'll need:

- lavender
- red or pink rose petals
- a cinnamon stick

- rosemary
- yarrow
- calendula
- rue
- lemongrass
- a small piece of paper
- a pencil
- a cloth pouch or bag, in red, orange, purple, or pink, long enough to hold a cinnamon stick
- Red string or yarn
- Three drops of Pure Love oil

In a bowl, mix the ingredients except for the cinnamon stick. On the slip of paper, write this sentence without lifting the pencil (don't worry if it looks sloppy, just do your best): *True Love, come to me.* Tightly roll the paper towards you. Place it against the cinnamon stick, and wrap the string or yarn around it tightly, three times. Say the Casting Words.

Place the herbs in the bowl into the pouch, carefully, then place the cinnamon stick wrapped with the paper. Add three drops of Pure Love oil and tie up the pouch.

Carry the pouch with you, or tie it to your bedpost for one lunar cycle.

## A Warm Heart In Winter Spell

What you'll need:

- two pine cones
- red string
- a fireplace or bonfire

Perform this spell on a waxing or full moon. Tie the pine cones together with the red string, and say "May I be united with my love by the next full moon." Say the Casting Words, then toss the pine cones into the fire to release the spell's energy into the universe.

## The Heart's Choice Divination Spell

What you'll need:

- two onions
- two pots and some potting soil
- a small, sharp knife
- collected rainwater
- a pink candle
- a candleholder or a small dish
- matches
- Pure Love oil
- a small, thin paintbrush

Do this on a new moon. After casting your circle, anoint the candle with the oil and light it. Take the knife and carefully inscribe the name of the two lovers you need guidance about—one in one onion, one in the other. As you carefully plant each onion, say the name of the lover in question.

Put one hand on each pot and call to the goddess:

"Wise and loving goddess, my heart is confused.

Help me know which lover I should choose.

With the first that grows, I will know."

Allow the candle to burn down, and once it has, water the soil well, then place the two pots where they can get the most sun. Whichever onion sprouts first, that is the lover you should choose.

**Rose Water Recipe**

What you'll need:

- rose petals, enough to fill a mason jar
- collected rain or river water
- cheesecloth
- a pink candle
- Pure Love oil
- a small, thin paintbrush

- matches
- a candleholder or small dish
- pink and white quartz
- a teaspoon of honey
- lemongrass
- honeysuckle blossoms
- one mint leaf

Do this spell on a new or waxing moon and finish it on a full moon. Anoint and light the pink candle. Place the lemongrass, mint leaf, honeysuckle blossoms, white and pink quartz and rose petals into the mason jar then fill to the brim with the collected water. Seal the jar.

Draw down the power of the moon and let it fill your circle as you hold the jar in your hands. Open your eyes when you imagine the moon energy glowing bright.

Say:

"A gentle brew I make for you,

to heal the heart and bring love true."

Imagine the loving energy from your own heart pouring into the jar. Give it three, firm shakes, then set it beside the candle.

Once the moon is visible, place the jar in a windowsill or outside where it can bask in the moon's light. On the night of the full moon, return the jar to your sacred workspace or altar. Say:

"By the light of the goddess moon,

I consecrate this spell to bring

true love soon."

Place it once again in the moonlight. The next day, carefully strain the rose water through a cheesecloth, setting the quartz stones aside to return to your altar for future use. Bottle the rose water to use in future love spells, to sprinkle on yourself before leaving the house if you seek true love, or to give as a gift to a friend who is looking for true love.

**A Spell to Strengthen Unconditional Love**

What you'll need:

- a black, pink, and white candle
- Sacred Oil blend: myrrh, frankincense, patchouli
- a small, thin paintbrush
- three small dishes or candleholders
- matches
- pink salt
- rose incense

After you cast your circle, anoint all three candles and set the pink candle in between the black and the white candles. Light them, then light the incense.

Draw a figure eight, beginning with the black candle, so that it crosses over the pink candle and encircles the black and white candles. Say:

"Balance divine, yours and mine

neverending, not pretending

strong and true, me and you

in this love, pure and fine."

Set the incense stick to burn in a holder, watch the smoke drift over the candles' flames as you imagine your love strengthening, becoming more balanced and stable. When you are ready, open the circle and allow the candles to burn down.

## Spells For Healing and Wellness

### White Light Healing Spell

What you'll need:

- a wall mirror
- a white pillar candle
- a dish or candleholder
- matches

- five white quartz pieces

You can do this spell at any time. The mirror doesn't have to be particularly large, just big enough that when you set it on the floor, against a wall, you can see your reflection if you're seated in front of it.

Place the mirror against a wall. Place the dish in front of it and set the candle on the dish; light the candle. Sit comfortably in front of the candle. Place the five quartz pieces around you on the floor so that you are surrounded by them. Allow your gaze to shift out of focus and watch your reflection in the mirror bathed in the light of the candle. Take deep, even breaths from your center—your shoulders should not move up and down, your belly should move in and out. Sit with good posture.

See the white, healing light combine with the natural aura of your body. Picture the white light brightening your aura, drawing out any negativity of illness from your body. Feel the healing, cool, white light comfort your body. Watch the new, white aura shimmer and glow. Stay in this state of mind for as long as it's comfortable.

When you are done, extinguish the candle by pinching the flame, and return the mirror to its place. You can do this as a simple meditation, or cast a circle to do it as a magical affirmation.

## Calming Waters Spell

What you'll need:

- a blue candle or bouquet of blue or white flowers

This is a spell that can be done in several places. You can perform it in the bathtub in your home, or in a lake, creek, river, or in the ocean. You don't need any spell ingredients but a candle for focus or a gift of flowers, and yourself, a body of water, and the elementals of water.

If taking a bath, cast a circle and light the candle for divine focus. If bathing in a natural body of water, leave the bouquet of flowers by the shore as thanks to the elementals of water.

This spell should be done on a dark or waning moon. Once submerged in the water, relax, take deep breaths. You can be standing or floating, or if in the bathtub, laying down. Once you've found that your mind is in a calm, healing place, say these words:

"Elementals of water, guardians of the rain

Elementals of water, fair spirits of the stream,

Elementals of water, children of Yemaya,

Elementals of water, shepherds of the sea,

Help me release all the worry, the stress,

the negative thoughts that trouble me.

Here in your safe, calming currents, I swim peacefully."

Feel the gentle embrace of the water, the push and pull of currents if you are in a natural body of water. Feel the cool, healing of the goddess and her elementals, surrounding you, comforting you, healing your pains, and worries. Remember that the goddess can handle all of the pain you release to her, she is infinite. Allow the stress to be taken from you. You are a child of the goddess, and she is a loving mother to all her children.

Take some of the water and wet the top of your head with it, thus anointing yourself. Feel the coolness of the water refresh your third eye and your crown chakra.

When you are ready, leave the water and allow the air to dry you, or pat yourself dry—do not wipe the healing water away.

**Healing Candle Spell**

What you'll need:

- a blue, white, or yellow candle
- Healing Oil: angelica, comfrey, and chamomile
- a small, thin paintbrush
- a dish or candleholder
- matches
- Tibetan healing incense
- an incense holder

- a small knife, or screw

Cast your circle and anoint the candle. With the small knife or screw tip, carve the words "heal me" in both sides of the candle, then light the candle. Light the incense and allow the smoke to drift across the candle flame, filling the room with a healing scent. (Place the incense far enough away from you so that you are not directly breathing the line of smoke). Allow your mind to drift into an alpha state: your gaze is out of focus, your mind is calm, thoughts are discarded as they enter the space of your mind. As the candle burns, know that you are in the right place for healing of the spirit, mind, body, and soul. Feel the benevolent energy fill your circle. Feel the power of the universe filling your circle with healing light.

When you are ready, open the circle and ground. Allow the candle and incense to burn down.

## Earth Cord Spell

This spell is a simple but powerfully effective one. On a full moon, find space to work unbothered and unobserved out of doors. Stand barefoot if you can but if the weather is cold or the ground too rough, shoes are fine.

Cast the circle around you and look up to the sky. Call the power of the sun or the moon into your circle, silently or out loud, and feel the energy of the universe slowly fill your sacred space until the space is completely filled with divine power.

Stand straight, with good posture, and breathe deeply, keeping your arms relaxed at your sides. Imagine a silver cord of energy going from your solar plexus, to your belly, down through your feet and deep into the Earth. Feel the exchange of energy from your body to the body of the goddess. With each breath, feel the healing coming up from the ground into your body.

At the same time, feel the negativity, stress, weariness, and worry leave your body through the silver cord, to be carried down into the Earth where it will be dissipated and cleansed, and renewed as bright, healing energy. Stay in this stance for as long as you need, allowing the goddess to heal your body, heart, and spirit.

**Burying a Bad Habit Healing Spell**

What you'll need:

- an egg
- a brown candle
- Tibetan healing incense
- Healing Oil
- a small, thin paintbrush
- a small dish or candleholder
- a shovel
- a brown paper bag

- a pencil

On a dark or waning moon, prepare your body first by bathing or showering. Cast your circle, and anoint the candle with Healing Oil. Light the candle as well as the Tibetan healing incense. Raise your hands to the sky and ask the god and goddess to grace your sacred circle with their healing energy. Imagine the circle filling with divine energy, and open your eyes when the energy glows the brightest.

Write on the paper bag the habit you wish to get rid of; be specific and detailed. Next, take the egg, and say:

"Little egg, a vehicle be

to remove the habit which vexes me,

so that I may see that habit undone

by the rise and set of the burning sun."

Now, take the egg, and slowly and gently rub it against you (careful not to break it!), starting with the top of your head, down to your face and neck, your shoulders and arms, your chest, ribs, and stomach, your lower back and buttocks, each leg and ankle, down to your feet and out over your toes. Place the egg carefully in the brown paper bag, and fold the bag so that it forms a small package. Move this package carefully and slowly, widdershins (counterclockwise), above the candle, careful not to get so close that the bag begins to burn. Say the Casting Words.

Open the circle and allow the candle and the incense to burn down while you go outside with the parcel and a shovel. Dig a small hole and bury the egg in the paper bag, and forget about it. In 24 hours' time, your bad habit should begin to dissipate, until it vanishes forever.

**Sunrise Affirmation Spell**

Perform this spell on a waxing, new, or full moon. Research at what time the sun will rise at your location. Make sure you get plenty of sleep the night before this spell. Set your alarm to wake you up with enough time to shower, drink some water, and feel refreshed and ready.

Stand facing East, preferably outdoors, but in front of an east-facing window is also permitted. As the sun rises, say:

"Like the sun,

each day I rise,

I will not stop,

nor compromise.

With each breathe,

I live and grow,

I will not stop,

onward, I go."

Feel the energy of the rising sun imbue you with strength, hope, and vitality. Make a commitment to do a sunrise affirmation once a month. The sunrise is a magical time, and being awake during it can be very healing for anyone, but especially those in the creative or healing arts. The dawn is a great source of inspiration, and of hope.

**Spells For The Home and Garden**

**House Blessings Jar**

What you'll need:

- a mason jar
- collected water such as rainwater or water from a river
- amethyst, white quartz, jade, and sunstone
- vervain
- comfrey
- rosemary
- alfalfa
- juniper berries
- any wildflowers that are growing on the property, such as dandelions
- honey

- some soil from outside the property, or the nearest park if the home is an apartment
- a coin of each denomination, including a silver dollar
- sage, palo santo, rosemary, or holy water (collected water and salt)
- sweet incense
- a yellow or green candle
- matches

Perform this spell on a new, waxing, or full moon. Especially powerful when performed on a blue moon (a second full moon in a month). Cast your circle around the entire home: if this is a house, you can walk around the outside of the house, or walk from room to room going north, east, south, then west.

Next, purge any negativity from the rooms using sage, palo santo wood, rosemary, or holy water. The holy water should be sprinkled in each room, walking widdershins about each room, all other ingredients should be lit so they smoke, and by holding them, making widdershins hand motions with the smoke in each room.

When you are finished cleansing the house, open the windows and doors, keeping an eye on small children and pets.

After a few minutes, close the windows and doors, and walk the house with the sweet incense, making sunwise hand movements to bless each room.

Finally, return to your altar and begin assembling the jar. Add the ingredients: soil and stones first, then coins, honey (save a little bit of the honey to anoint the candle), herbs, wildflowers, and last, water. Seal the jar.

Melt the bottom of the candle to affix it to the lid of the mason jar. Anoint the candle with the remaining honey, then light the candle.

Say:

"Bless this house,

this cozy home,

a place of peace,

back home to come,

let good luck grow

and bless these rooms,

let happiness flow,

often and soon,

peace to this home,

and who dwell within,

where love and light,

come pouring in,

by day and night,

through thick and thin,

this house is blessed,

and all within."

Allow the candle to burn down, and open the circle. Light another candle on the jar whenever you wish to reactivate it, on a full or new moon, reciting the words.

**House Cleansing Ritual**

What you'll need:

- a household broom or magic besom
- Florida or holy water
- kosher salt and pepper

On a dark or waxing moon, and after securing all pets and small children, open the exterior doors of your house. Sprinkle Florida water or holy water lightly on the floor in front of you, and sweep it towards the doors, beginning in the center of the house. You can put the water in a spray bottle to lightly mist the floors, especially if there is carpet. Do this in each room until you're in the rooms that lead to the outside, and continue sweeping until you reach the thresholds. Sprinkle a small amount of salt and pepper on the thresholds, then sweep the water, salt and pepper outside, taking with it all the negative energy that's been tracked in.

Take care to thoroughly sweep the salt and pepper so nobody tracks it back in, and pets don't carry it on their paws. Another approach is to sew small cloth packets of salt and pepper mixture and place these on the thresholds to ceremoniously collect the negative energy to sweep out of the house.

**Garden Blessing Spell**

What you'll need:

- white quartz flakes

Do this spell on a new, waxing, or full moon. It is best done in the morning or in the evening, whenever your garden is in shade and when you typically water your plants. At your altar, set a pitcher of water and light a white candle. Cast your circle and call down the energies of the sun and the moon, and ask them to fill the water with their healing light. Open the circle and carry your pitcher out to the garden, bringing with you a pocket of quartz flakes. Water your plants as you would, then take each flake and set it a couple of inches into the soil among your plants, pouring the blessed water on top of it as you work. When you are finished, say:

"With blessings of the moon and sun,

my garden grows, one by one."

**Spells For Protection**

**Front Door Protection Charm**

What you'll need:

- a clove of garlic
- red cloth bag
- three needles or pins
- rosemary
- sage
- Crown of Success oil or Dragon's Blood oil
- African violet petals
- twine
- scissors

On a Tuesday or Saturday of a dark or waning moon, cast your circle and press the pins carefully through the clove of garlic. Carefully place the garlic into the cloth bag, and add to this the rosemary, sage, garlic, African violet petals, and six drops of oil. Close the bag and wrap it three times in twine, making a loop from which you can hang the bag on or near the front door.

Hold the bag towards the moon, and say:

"From this moment, from this hour,

trouble keep far from my door,

I use my cunning and my power,

to keep that which would harm me far away, forevermore."

Say the Casting Words. Affix the bag to the front door, or close to it. Recharge it twice a year with six additional drops of oil, and repeat the incantation.

**Witch's Jar**

What you'll need:

- a mason jar or any household food jar that once held something sour, such as pickles, or sauerkraut
- a collection of rusted, metal objects: screws, nails, hooks, etc.
- broken glass (not mirrors)
- vinegar
- a lock of your own hair, and some of your fingernail clippings
- a black candle
- matches
- a candleholder or small plate

A witch's jar performs a simple function. Interestingly, it was once believed that one could trap a witch within such a jar—

today, however, the witch's jar is a way to trap negativity, ill will, and animosity that's directed towards you.

On a dark or waning moon, light the black candle and place everything from the list inside the jar. Seal the jar and drip some of the wax from the candle on the lid, and say:

"All that serves to harm me, come inside this jar and stay."

Snuff out the candle and take the jar outside to bury it. Some witches make four jars in total, one for each side of the house. If you rent or live in an apartment or any home without a yard, you can place the witch's jar in a pot of gardening soil. You can even place a live plant in the pot—perfect camouflage for your jar!

**Four Corners House Protection Spell**

What you'll need:

- four black cloth bags
- four small, circular mirrors
- twine
- kosher salt
- black peppercorns

Remember that black is an important color in protection magic and should not be considered "evil" or "dark". Just as the darkness of night protects animals who need protection against predators so do we sometimes use the color black to keep us hidden from our enemies.

Cast a circle on a dark or waning moon. Place inside each cloth bag a mirror, a pinch of kosher salt and a pinch of black peppercorns. Tie up the bags and bind them each three times with twine, making a loop in one of the binds so the bag can be hung, if you choose. Hold each bag in your hand and say for each one:

"Invisible to misfortune,

my home remains a safe haven.

Invisible to trouble,

my home remains safe,

behind a black wing, like the raven."

Place one bag on each side of your house. You can hang it from a window or place it on the ground, whichever you prefer.

## Invisible From Harm Personal Protection Spell

What you'll need:

- a fresh basil leaf
- a dime
- a piece of onyx
- white yarn, or any thick, white thread.
- Crown of Success oil

- a small, sharp knife or boline
- a black candle
- a white candle
- two candleholders or two small dishes
- matches

On a dark, new, or waning moon, cast your circle. Carefully carve the words "Trouble do not see me" on each candle. Place the candles on your altar, one candle to each side of you, and the ingredients in the middle. Take the basil leaf and place the dime upon it, then the piece of onyx upon that. Carefully wrap the three items together with the yarn or thread, concentrating on being able to walk about in the world, free from harm, not troubled by others. When you are finished, tie three knots while you say:

"Trouble do not see me." Say the Casting Words.

Carry this charm in your pocket, backpack, briefcase or purse to keep harm from finding you.

**Safe Journeys Spell**

What you'll need:

- a white rose (only the flower, removes the stem)
- a white feather
- a white cloth bag

- a lodestone
- nag champa incense
- matches

A lodestone can be purchased in a pagan supplies shop or online. Do this spell during any lunar phase but the dark moon. After you cast your circle, light the incense. Hold the white rose blossom and circle it sunwise with the incense, then place it in the bag. Do the same for the white feather, and for the lodestone. Tie up the bag and hold it up, then circle it three more times with the incense. Say:

"May this blessed charm, filled with light,

bring safe travels, day and night."

You can make this charm for a loved one or friend who's planning on traveling, or for yourself before a trip. You can also keep it in your car to keep you safe while you drive on daily errands or your commute.

As with all charms, you can recharge this one under a full moon when you feel the need to.

**Invisible Ward Spell**

What you'll need:

- kosher salt

- collected water, such as rainwater or river water.
- obsidian
- a black candle
- Crown of Success oil
- a small, thin paintbrush
- a small glass, or your cauldron or cup
- a small knife or your boline

Do this spell under a dark moon. After you cast the circle, carve a figure eight symbol in the black candle, and anoint it with the Crown of Success oil. Fill the container you've chosen to use with the collected water, then add a teaspoon of salt. Take the piece of obsidian, and make a figure eight symbol in the air directly above the container of water.

Say:

"Infinity circles, day and night,

charge this water

to keep me out of sight."

Drop the obsidian into the water. Place the cup outside or in the windowsill to soak up the dark moon's energy. Allow the candle to burn down.

Keep the invisibility water in a bottle or spill-proof container. When you want to use it, either paint a small figure eight on your body (good places are your chest or stomach, anywhere where the salt residue won't be seen), or on your front door, or vehicle, depending upon the context of your need for invisibility.

**Spells For Luck**

Birthday Blessings Spell

What you'll need:

- a tall white pillar or taper candle
- a small, sharp knife or your boline
- Altar oil: frankincense, rose, lemongrass
- Florida water
- a small, thin paintbrush
- a small dish or candleholder
- matches

Do this spell on your birthday, regardless of lunar phase. If it occurs on a waning moon, be prepared for unnecessary or harmful things to begin to move out of your life, so that the happiness can move in.

Cast your circle and carefully carve two-word wishes into the candle, such as: "gentle love", "happy home", or "satisfying work". Use your imagination and carve what you truly want for the coming year. Anoint the candle with the altar oil. Light the candle. Take the Florida water and place a small amount on the top of your head, your forehead, the back of your neck, and on the back of your hands.

Gaze at the candle's flame, and imagine scenes in which the things you've carved occur, or could occur. Take deep, calming breaths from your stomach, and sit with a straight posture. Take some time in this sacred space, breathing, and meditating on the happy year you have in front of you. Even if you've recently suffered a trauma or loss, imagine the year bringing you healing, and solace from the pain.

When you are ready, open the circle and ground, but allow the candle to burn down on its own.

**Nutmeg Spell**

What you'll need:

- a whole nutmeg
- frankincense oil
- a dollar bill
- red string or yarn

Do this spell on a full moon. Cast your circle, and hold the nutmeg in your hand as you call upon the energy of the moon to fill your sacred spice with lunar energy. Dab a bit of frankincense oil on the nutmeg, then wrap it in the dollar bill. Next, bind the wrapped nutmeg in red string, seven times. Tie the knot three times, and say:

"Lucky charm, bold and bright,

bring me luck both day and night."

Allow the charm to bask in the light of the full moon, then carry it on your person, bag, car, or altar.

## Seven Berries Spell

What you'll need:

- seven juniper berries
- a small green or white bag

Begin this spell on a Sunday during a waxing moon—making sure that the full moon is at least seven days away. Cast your circle and place the juniper berries in the bag. Hold it in your hands and allow the power of the sun and the moon to fill your circle, and charge the berries.

Carry the berries on you for seven days. After that, discard them in running water. You will then have a very lucky week.

## Help With Legal Issues Spell

What you'll need:

- red jasper
- hematite

- small white cloth bag
- High John the Conqueror root
- Success oil: basil, myrrh, dragon's blood, rosemary
- small, thin paintbrush
- the Justice tarot card
- the World tarot card
- the Empress tarot card
- a small, yellow candle
- matches
- a candleholder or small dish
- a red apple

Do this spell on a waxing or full moon, on a Monday or a Friday. Before you begin, thoroughly cleanse yourself both physically and spiritually. Smudge your altar space and tools.

Anoint the candle and light it. Allow its warm glow to soothe your anxiety about the upcoming court case or legal issue.

Take the High John root, which can be purchased online or in a magical supply store, and consecrate it with the success oil. Hold it to your forehead and say:

"Justice be gentle, and favor me,

Empress be loving, and comfort me,

World be open for me to journey,

may things go my way, successfully."

Place the High John root in the bag. Stand the three cards up behind the candle or on the altar so you can gaze at them. Take the red jasper in your left hand, the hematite in your right, and look at the cards, one at a time, as you repeat:

"Justice be gentle, and favor me,

Empress be loving, and comfort me,

World be open for me to journey,

may things go my way, successfully."

Place the jasper and hematite in the bag and tie it securely. Now take the Justice card and place it on top of the bag. Say:

"Justice, find all in favor of me that I will be successful in my endeavors." Return that card to the altar.

Take the Empress card and place it on top of the bag. Say:

"Empress, mother goddess, soothe my fears and let those who I deal with have mercy on me." Return that card to the altar.

Take the World card and place it on top of the bag. Say:

"Universe, enable it so that I keep my liberty and dignity, and am allowed to walk my path uninhibited in this World." Return that card to the altar.

When you are finished, allow the candle to burn down. Take the remaining wax and the apple and place in a crossroads at your earliest convenience.

# Conclusion

Thank for making it through to the end of *Wicca Spells*. Let's hope it was informative and able to provide you with all of the tools you need to achieve your goals whatever they may be. Through this book, you learned a bit on the origin and history of Wicca, its beliefs and practices, some of the tools used by Wiccans, the elements and the Wheel of the Year, and how to perform spells. Among the spells included in this book are those that attract luck in wealth, money, love, as well as protection of home and safe travels.

The next step is to begin to research what you want out of magic. Do you want to change your life? If so, how? Start with small details and see if one area of your life needs more attention than the rest. Once you've decided what aspect you'd like to focus your first spell upon, start to look up the phases of the moon, the times of sunrise and sunset where you live, and which days of the week would be best to perform this spell. See what ingredients are needed, and go about collecting them. Take your time, and enjoy the process of preparing to cast your first spell.

Once you're ready to create magic, remember to relax and have fun with it. A mistake is not a dealbreaker—whatever you do, do so with good, strong intent, and you will see the results better than you imagined.

You may instead choose to pick a spell in this book and just go for it. That's okay too! Curiosity in magic leads to miraculous things. Learning keeps us alive and filled with the energy of the god and goddess. So, test the waters, explore, be brave—and know that every spell in this book has been crafted with the new witch in mind.

Finally, if you want to go slow and gradually build your altar, gather and purchase your tools, grow a magical herb garden, and wait until the time is right for you to delve into the world of Wiccan magic, that is okay, too. There is no wrong way to honor yourself in Wicca. Choose the path that's right for you.

Finally, if you found this book useful in any way, a review on Amazon is always appreciated!

CPSIA information can be obtained
at www.ICGtesting.com
Printed in the USA
LVHW031817220120
644443LV00012B/680